DERBYS

FOLK
TALES

DERBYSHIRE
FOLK
TALES

PETE CASTLE

ILLUSTRATED BY RAY ASPDEN

The
History
Press

To all the tellers who told these tales before me, and to all those who will carry them on into the future.

First published 2010

Reprinted 2011

The History Press
The Mill, Brimscombe Port
Stroud, Gloucestershire, GL5 2QG
www.thehistorypress.co.uk

British Library Cataloguing in Publication Data.
A catalogue record for this book is available from the British Library.

ISBN 978 0 7524 5388 0

Typesetting and origination by The History Press
Printed in Great Britain

CONTENTS

Acknowledgements

Thanks to:

Sue for sticking with me for the past forty-plus years and for reading and criticising the rough drafts

Bob Trubshaw for being the go-between with The History Press

Ray for the pictures

All the musicians and storytellers I've worked with over the years

And, especially, all the people who have listened to me tell stories and sing songs for over three decades. I don't like to call you 'fans', but I suppose you are.

THE DERBY RAM

From almost anywhere in Belper, where I live, I am aware of the hills which loom over the town. They are called the Chevin (Cefn: from Old British or Brithonic/Celtic word for a wooded ridge) and they are one of my favourite places. I love walking there. North Lane, variously described as a Roman road or packhorse route, is like a time warp; you can imagine yourself back into distant history and when you come down off the hills you find a whole network of pathways leading towards the town and the mills. They always bring to my mind stories and songs, including some of those in this book.

It's odd that I should be writing a book of Derbyshire folk tales for I am, by birth, a man of Kent. However, I left that county when I went to Bretton Hall College of Education in the West Riding of Yorkshire, as it was then called, in 1965 and haven't lived there since. After short spells in Lincolnshire and Nottingham and a longer period in Luton, we came to Derbyshire over twenty years ago and I now definitely think of it as 'home'.

It was whilst living in Luton in 1978 that I gave up my 'proper' job as a teacher to go full time as a folk musician, a thing I had been doing as a hobby and then semi-professionally ever since college. Some time soon after that I discovered storytelling and have divided my time pretty equally between the two ever since. In fact, I describe myself as 'a storyteller who sings half his stories', and I rarely do a performance which does not include at least a token number of both forms.

When we moved to Derby in 1987 I told myself that I would not learn any Derbyshire songs or stories, partly because I didn't want to step on the toes of those who were already doing them, but mainly because of the problem of accent and dialect. I don't 'do' dialect anyway but, coming from the south, I speak of 'bath' and 'grass' with a long 'ar' sound in the middle, as in the word 'marvellous', whereas locals use a short 'a', as in 'happy'. That doesn't particularly matter in stories but it sometimes affects the rhymes in songs. Another worry was 'authenticity'. Could, and should, I do Derbyshire material, not being a native?

I gave in because, like most storytellers, I do quite a lot of work in schools and I realised that most of the local schoolchildren had not heard of 'The Derby Ram'. They all supported the local football team, Derby County, but had no idea why their nickname was 'the Rams'. Soon I discovered that, outside of the folk scene, many of the adults did not have a great deal more knowledge. People who had lived in the city their whole lives did not associate with the song despite the bells of the cathedral playing a version of the tune. A few older ones remembered singing it when they were at school, but it was the exception to find anyone who knew anything else about it. (It was one of the first folk songs I was ever aware of, from way back before I became interested in folk music *per se* and was still at school in Kent. My first version was probably sung by Burl Ives.)

Now I always try to include it when I work in Derbyshire. That led on to other songs and then I found some stories and that gave rise to this book. So, to thank 'The Derby Ram', we'll start with that.

Although 'The Derby Ram' is not actually a story, it is the iconic image of Derbyshire. As a song, 'The Derby Ram' is known throughout the English speaking world. There are versions from all over the British Isles, not just Derbyshire, and it made itself at home in America, Canada, Australia, New Zealand – wherever English people made their homes. It also crops up in poetry anthologies, particularly those aimed at children, although it is by no means childish (some verses in some versions are very adult!).

The 'story' which all these versions tell is pretty much the same: as I was going to Derby I chanced upon an enormous ram… there is then a catalogue of the different parts of the ram, how big they were and what was, or could be, done with them. End of story. Although the words stay pretty constant, the tunes and choruses vary widely.

Here is a typical set of words collected by Llewellynn Jewitt in the mid-nineteenth century:

The Derby Ram

As I was going to Darby (sic), Sir,
All on a market day,
I met the finest Ram, Sir,
That ever was fed on hay.

Daddle-i-day, daddle-i-day,
Fal-de-ral, fal-de-ral, diddle-i-day.

This Ram was fat behind, Sir,
This Ram was fat before,
This Ram was ten yards high, Sir,
Indeed he was no more.

The wool upon his back, Sir,
Reached up unto the sky,
The eagles made their nests there, Sir,
For I heard the young ones cry.

The wool upon his belly, Sir,
It dragged upon the ground,
It was sold in Darby town, Sir,
For forty thousand pound.

The space between his horns, Sir,
Was as far as a man could reach,
And there they built a pulpit
For the parson there to preach.

The teeth that were in his mouth, Sir,
Were like a regiment of men,
And the tongue that hung between them, Sir,
Would have dined them twice and again.

This Ram jumped o'er a wall, Sir,
His tail caught on a briar,
It reached from Darby town, Sir,
All into Leicestershire.

And of this tail so long, Sir,
Twas ten miles and an ell,
They made a goodly rope, Sir,
To toll the market bell.

This Ram had four legs to walk on, Sir,
This Ram had four legs to stand,
And every leg he had, Sir,
Stood on an acre of land.

The butcher that killed this Ram, Sir,
Was drownded in the blood,
And the boy that held the pail, Sir,
Was carried away in the flood.

All the maids in Darby, Sir,
Came begging for his horns,
To take them to coopers,
To make them milking gawns.

The little boys of Darby, Sir,
They came to beg his eyes,
To kick about the streets, Sir,
For they were football size.

The tanner that tanned its hide, Sir,
Would never be poor any more,
For when he had tanned and retched it,
It covered all Sinfin Moor.

The jaws that were in his head, Sir,
They were so fine and thin,
They were sold to a Methodist parson,
For a pulpit to preach in.

Indeed, Sir, this is true, Sir,
I never was taught to lie,
And had you been to Darby, Sir,
You'd have seen it as well as I.

What else is there to know? Well, in addition to the song, 'The Derby Ram' is part of a mummer's-type play often called *The Owd Tup*. This play was (and still is in a few places) performed around Christmas time, mainly in the north-east of the county, around Chesterfield and up into South Yorkshire and Sheffield. The play is very simple – a farmer and his wife have a ram and they are looking for a butcher to kill it. After various introductory speeches we get:

Farmer:	Hey! Our old lass, is there a butcher in the town?
Wife:	My brother Bill's a blacksmith.
Farmer:	I said a butcher. Open thee ears, thee blockhead.
Wife:	Oh, our Bob's a butcher.
Farmer:	Well, fetch him here to stick this tup.
Wife:	Bob! Bob! Come and stick this tup.

After a bit of horseplay Bob does 'stick' the tup, which falls down dead and the hat is passed round. Various verses of the song are usually sung at places within the play.

Nobody knows for sure where, when or why either the song or the play first came about. They have definitely been known for several hundred years and various folklorists have surmised that they go back far longer, and might possibly even be a survival from Viking settlers or pre-Roman Britons. Sydney Oldall Addy, who will crop up again later in the book, wrote the following:

Amongst the earliest recollections of my childhood is the performance of the 'Derby Ram,' or, as we used to call it, the Old Tup. With tile eye of memory I can see a number of young men standing one winter's evening in the deep porch of an old country house, and singing the ballad of the Old Tup. In the midst of the company was a young man with a sheep's skin, horns and all, on his back, and standing on all fours. What it all meant I could not make out, and the thing that most impressed me was the roar of the voices in that vault-like porch…

And elsewhere:

Now when I first read the Edda, and came to the passage which tells how the sons of Bor slew the giant Ymir, and how, when he fell, so much blood ran out of his wounds that all the race of frost-giants was drowned in it, I said to myself, 'Why, that's the "Old Tup" and when I read further on and found how they made the sea from his blood, the earth from his flesh, the rocks from his teeth, the heaven from his skull, it seemed to me that I had guessed rightly. The Old Tup was the giant Ymir, and the mummers of my childhood were acting the drama of the Creation.

So perhaps in 'The Derby Ram' we have an ancient Scandinavian creation myth still regularly re-enacted in the heart of England! Another theory I have recently come across, and like, is that it is an Anglo-Saxon import. Very similar rituals took place all over Germany up until the end of the nineteenth century. That would also explain the identical happenings in Transylvania too, where many Germans settled in the Middle Ages. Either way, it would make it the oldest item in this collection, although others go back a long way too. Several are legends dating back to the time of the Normans or beyond; King Arthur makes an appearance and Robin Hood, arguably the greatest English folk hero, features several times. At the other end of the spectrum, one story probably has its origins in a nineteenth-century short story and another may have begun as a story told in a school assembly! There are also the Derbyshire versions of several classic fairy tales of the sort which might be found in the collections of Grimm or Perrault, and some tall tales which are pretty timeless.

Whatever their origins, at one time or another they have almost all been told orally before being collected and written down. I hope that the oral aspect will continue – that you might tell some of them. I have told some of them for many years and will be telling others in the future.

For this book I have tried to walk that difficult tightrope between the informal colloquialisms of an oral telling and a literary reworking. I expect I've slipped to one side or the other on several occasions. A literal transcription of the oral telling does not read well on the page where the gestures, facial expressions and asides are lacking. Also, many tellings are in places, or to audiences, which make certain explanations and descriptions unnecessary, although they add to the story on the page.

So these are stories intended for telling and they are presented as such, not as academic texts. They may have changed in quite fundamental ways from the version I first came across. They might not be historically correct, but they are good stories!

Pete Castle
Belper, 2010

ONE

TALES OF LOVE
AND LOVERS

This is one of the longest sections in this book and some of the other stories could have been included here too. You could almost say that most traditional stories deal with love (or its opposite) in one form or another.

Here we have tales of true love, tales where love conquers against all difficulties, thwarted love and lovers betrayed.

Most of the best love songs and stories have some element of distress in them, as shown by the apocryphal story of the pop star who went to his manager full of anguish and broken hearted and told him 'My woman has run off with my best friend!' The manager rubbed his hands and said, 'So we'll be getting some good new songs for the next album then!'

LIKE MEAT LOVES SALT

I am often asked, 'What is your favourite story?' I usually reply that I like them all or I wouldn't tell them, but there are some for which I definitely have a soft spot. This is one of my favourite Derbyshire stories – and probably one of my favourites out of all that I tell.

It started as a very short fragment, so when I decided to tell it I had to complete it and since then it has grown in repeated tellings. It is a strange but lovely tale which starts like *King Lear* but finishes like *Cinderella*! The ending is guaranteed to get an 'Aaah!' from the audience.

There was once a man who had three daughters and one day he did one of those things which no one in their right mind would do – he sat his daughters down and he asked them each in turn how much they loved him. Now you'd know that was going to lead to trouble wouldn't you? Somebody was sure to get hurt!

First he turned to his eldest daughter and said, 'How much do you love me, my dear?'

She replied, 'Father, I love you more then the sun and the moon and the stars and the universe and everything!' And that pleased him.

Then he turned to his middle daughter, 'How much do you love me, my dear?'

'Father, I love you more than I love my own life', she said. And that pleased him too.

So then it was the turn of his youngest daughter, and his youngest daughter was really his favourite even though he didn't like to admit it – even to himself. 'How much do you love me, my dear?' he asked.

She thought for a while and then said, 'Father, I love you like meat loves salt'. And he didn't understand that at all.

'Meat? Salt? We have meat every day', he thought. 'Salt?

You can buy a big block of salt for a few pence… You don't love me at all, you ungrateful girl. Get out! Go away! I never want to see you again!' he shouted, and he banished her there and then from his house, with just the clothes she was wearing.

She wandered across the countryside until she came across a young gentleman who had been out riding and had had an accident. He'd been thrown from his horse and was lying on the ground more dead than alive. She was able to go and fetch water from a stream and revive him.

When he opened his eyes, he didn't know where he was and he didn't remember what had happened. All he was aware of was a beautiful face bending over him and comforting him and he knew that this creature had saved his life. He didn't know who it was, or what it was. Was it a fairy or a wood nymph? Had he died and gone to Heaven? Was it an angel? Or was it a young woman? Whoever, or whatever, she was, he instantly fell deeply in love with her and he took the ring from his finger and gave it to her.

As soon as she saw that he was going to be alright, she gathered up her skirts and ran off, leaving the young gentleman to gather his wits and climb back on his horse and turn its head towards his home.

The horse knew the way and with every step it took, the young man fell more and more deeply in love with the mysterious young woman who had saved his life. So much so that when he got home all he could do was to take to his bed and stay there dying of love-sickness. He couldn't eat, he couldn't sleep, he didn't wash himself or comb his hair. He could think of nothing but the young woman.

He lay there with that hollow, empty feeling in his chest as though his heart had been wrenched out and his whole self with it.

Who was the mysterious young woman he was in love with? How was he going to find her again? That was all he could think about.

Meanwhile... she wandered across the countryside for several more days until she came to a big house and she plucked up the courage to go to the back door and beg a bite of food to eat and some water to drink; and because the people were kind to her she dared to ask whether there was a job going, for now she was banished from her father's house she had to find some way of supporting herself. She was given a job as the lowliest kitchen maid, the skivvy; the one who had to get up first in the morning to light the fires to heat the water before anyone else got up; the one that had all the dirtiest pots and pans to clean out. It wasn't what she was used to but it wasn't too bad.

Over the next few days, just by listening to what the other servants were gossiping about, she pieced together the story that somewhere upstairs in the house was the young master who had had an accident when he was out riding. His life had been saved by some mysterious young woman whom he had fallen madly in love with, and now he was dying of a broken heart and no one could think of a way to find the young woman and so save his life and make him happy.

The next time the cook prepared some broth for the invalid, the young woman persuaded the 'tweeny', the servant who usually did the running up and down stairs, to let her take it up to the young man. She quickly wiped her face and hands but couldn't get rid of all the dirt and grime which had built up. As she was going up the stairs she slipped the ring he had given to her into the bowl.

The young invalid wasn't interested in broth, he wasn't interested in anything except finding his true love, but she persuaded him that he had to have a little of the soup. He ate a couple of mouthfuls without thinking and then the spoon clinked on something in the bottom of the bowl. He fished it out. It was his ring, the one he had given to the girl in the forest. 'Where did you get this ring?' he demanded.

'From him who it belongs to', she answered.

Up to this point he hadn't taken any notice of the servant girl who had brought the soup. (Those of you who have servants know that they are invisible, just like pieces of furniture!) But at that he stopped and looked at her, and he saw through the dirt and the grime. They fell into each other's arms and before many minutes had passed a wedding had been arranged!

As the bride at the wedding it was her privilege to arrange the food, so she told the cook that she didn't mind what was served but that it must all be prepared without any salt.

'I can't do that!' spluttered the cook. 'Just think what everyone would say. No one would eat it. It would be horrible! I have my reputation to think of. I'm a good cook and people recognise that. I won't do it!' But the bride insisted.

On the day of the wedding everyone from all around was invited, including the man with three daughters with

whom we started the story. He knew who the groom was
to be and felt honoured to have been asked to the wedding, but he had no idea about the identity of the bride.
When the ceremony was over everyone took their places
in the great hall for the wedding feast. There were rows
and rows of tables and the guests were arranged along
them in order of importance. At the front of the hall, at
right angles to the others, was the table for the wedding

party. When everyone was seated the food was served and everyone started to eat, but after a few mouthfuls the room began to hum with the sound of grumbling and complaining. There was a great deal of spluttering and grimacing. 'There's no salt in the food!', 'What's the cook thinking of?', 'We can't eat this...' Then, amidst all the complaining and mumbling, an old man seated at the back of the room stood up and let out a loud wail, 'O woe is me!' he cried. 'Once upon a time I had a daughter and I asked her how much she loved me and she said she loved me like meat loves salt. I didn't understand what she meant and I sent her away. She's probably been taken by bandits or eaten by wild beasts and I'll never see her again...'

Everyone was shocked and the room fell silent. Then the young bride rose to her feet and walked down the room and embraced her father. And the two of them were reconciled.

And they all lived happily ever after.

THE GOLDEN BALL
OR HANGMAN

Like the previous story this one was collected by Sydney Oldall Addy. Mr Addy lived at the end of the nineteenth century in Norton, which was then a separate village in Derbyshire but is now a suburb to the south-west of Sheffield. He was a very clever and interesting man. I have no idea what he did for a living – I have heard someone describe him as the Revd Addy but I don't think that is correct – but, in the way of the times, he was an expert amateur at no end of things. He collected and wrote about folk songs and customs, traditional stories, archaeology, buildings, children's games; in fact anything which he found interesting and worth preserving.

One of the – no, I think *the* – best ever collection of Derbyshire folk tales is the one he published in 1895 called *Household Tales and Traditional Remains* which is, sadly, impossible to get hold of these days but can be found in various libraries and archives. Addy said it was a collection of stories he found in the counties of York, Lincoln, Derby and Nottingham. However, an analysis of the places he credits for the stories put almost all of them, apart from the Lincolnshire ones, within the small area where those three counties meet. In other words, within a short distance of his home in Norton. I don't now how he travelled, probably by horse or pony and trap – I don't suppose an antiquarian would go in for one of those new-fangled automobiles! I like to picture him on his bicycle, peddling out across the moors heading for the Hope Valley or to Chesterfield armed with his notebooks and wondering what gems he would find that day.

This strange little story was told to him by Sarah Ellen Potter, aged fourteen, 'the daughter of Mr George Potter, of Castleton' (who, I believe, may have kept one of the pubs in the town). 'Hangman' is well known as a song. It is one of the classic ballads and has been sung by all kinds of folk singers, including the black American blues singer Leadbelly and the rock band Led Zeppelin!

Once upon a time there was a little girl. She was a nice little girl and everyone loved her, including the Magician. One day the Magician created for her a beautiful golden ball and he gave it to her father to present to her on her birthday. But along with the ball went a warning – if you ever lose the ball, the Magician will have you hanged!

One day her parents were going out and they told her all the things that parents always tell children before they go – about being good and not doing anything she shouldn't do, or going anywhere she shouldn't go, or speaking to strangers, and they reminded her of the warning the Magician had given her: do not lose your golden ball!

The parents went away and the little girl went out to play and she took her golden ball with her because she loved to play with it, to feel the weight of it, and the coolness of it, and to watch it as it rolled through the grass and reflected the colours of the sky and the flowers.

As she was playing with the ball it rolled into the stream behind the Magician's house and she could not find it. When she returned home, the Magician was waiting for her and he took her away and locked her in the dungeon of his house, while outside, they built the gallows on which to hang her.

That night her father came to visit her and she said:

> O hangman, hangman, stay thy hand
> A little before I die,
> I think I see my father coming,
> Hastening through yonder sty.

> O father hast thou brought my ball,
>   Or hast thou bought me free?
> Or art thou come to see me hung
>   Upon the gallows-tree?

Her father replied:

> I have not brought thy ball, my dear,
>   I have not bought thee free,
> But I have come to see thee hung
>   Upon the gallows-tree.

Her father went away, sadly, and the little girl began to cry. Then her mother came to visit her and the girl said:

> O hangman, hangman, stay thy hand
>   A little before I die,
> I think I see my mother coming,
>   Hastening through yonder sty.
> O mother hast thou brought my ball,
>   Or hast thou bought me free?
> Or art thou come to see me hung
>   Upon the gallows-tree?

Her mother replied:

> I have not brought thy ball, my dear,
>   I have not bought thee free,
> But I have come to see thee hung
>   Upon the gallows-tree.

Her mother embraced her and explained that she could do nothing to save her for it was the Magician's rule and, with tears rolling down her face, she went away.

After that the little girl was visited by her brothers and her sisters and her cousins and all her neighbours and she asked them all the same question and they all gave her the same reply and said they were unable to set her free.

When she had given up all hope and was expecting to be hanged the next morning, there came a loud knocking at the door and the gaoler admitted a young man – her true love.

> O hangman, hangman, stay thy hand
> A little before I die,
> I think I see my true love coming,
> Hastening through yonder sty.
> O true love hast thou brought my ball,
> Or hast thou bought me free?
> Or art thou come to see me hung
> Upon the gallows-tree?

Her true love bent and kissed her and said:

> O I have brought thy ball, my dear,
> And I have bought thee free,
> And I have brought a coach and six
> To take thee away with me.

And the true love reached into a bag he was carrying and brought out the golden ball, and he returned it to the Magician, and the gaoler set the little girl free and together she and her true love climbed into the coach and six and drove off into the sunset.

MR FOX
OR OVERHEARD UP A TREE

In folklore there are two stories which share the title 'Mr Fox'. The best known is a fairy tale related to the French 'Bluebeard'. In it a young woman marries and goes to live in her husband's castle. He is called Mr Fox, although he is

a normal human being with no obviously foxy character-
istics. When he is called away on business he gives his wife
the keys to the castle and tells her she can go anywhere
except for one particular room. Of course she does go into
that room – well, you would wouldn't you? There she finds
the rotting corpses of her husband's previous wives. In different versions, her trespassing is discovered in different
ways, but she is always found out. Sometimes it is a blood
stain which won't be removed, sometimes she takes the
initiative and tells Mr Fox about finding the room herself,
pretending it was in a dream. I think I am safe in saying
that she always escapes and Mr Fox is usually chopped into
pieces by her brothers!

Most versions of that story contain a rhyme which goes:

> Be bold, be bold,
> But not too bold,
> Lest that your heart's blood,
> Should run cold!

Addy did collect a very fragmentary version of that story,
but this 'Mr Fox' is much more domestic and happens in
a much more identifiable time and environment. I think
you can see a distant genetic link though.

Mary was about fifteen years old, on the cusp between
being a girl and a young woman. She had left school about
a year ago, as most girls did in those days, and had been
lucky enough to get herself a job as a maid-of-all-work
on a farm not too far from home. I say 'lucky enough'
because when you got a job at the Hiring Fair as Mary

had done, you never knew quite what it was going to be like. Sometimes employers were cruel and treated young girls almost like slaves – or worse. But Mary's employers treated her well, almost like one of the family – the daughter they didn't have. Most of her time was spent helping the farmer's wife in the house – dusting and cleaning and cooking, or around the farm yard, collecting eggs, sometimes milking the cows. Rarely was she asked to do heavy work out in the fields, just at harvest time or when a job needed doing urgently and they were short-handed. Mary had enjoyed the time she had spent on the farm and, now the year was drawing near its end, she was hoping that she would be taken on again next year.

In all the time Mary had spent on the farm she had only been home once and that was on Mothering Sunday, when everybody tried to get home if they possibly could. Now Mary was looking forward to going home again. And there were several reasons she was particularly looking forward to it apart from just the joy of seeing her parents and her brothers and sisters again. One of the main ones was that she would be taking her wages home with her. Although this would only be a few pounds, Mary knew that it would be a big help with the family budget and she was proud that she could contribute. It made her feel grown-up. The other thing that Mary was excited about was that she was going to be accompanied on her walk home by Matthew.

Matthew was a young man she had met a short while ago at the Harvest Supper. He was working on a neighbouring farm. He was a bit older than Mary but they had hit it off straight away. They'd danced together and talked and giggled. Since then they'd managed to meet a few times, just briefly, at the stile in the boundary wall between their two properties. The last time they'd met they had made the arrangement that Matthew would escort her home. He had said that he didn't like the idea of her walking all that way alone, particularly with the money with her. Mary was flattered that he wanted to take care of her. He was her first boyfriend.

Matthew and Mary had arranged that they would meet at the stile on the last afternoon of her work, but things did not quite go to plan. Being good, kind people, Mary's employers let her finish early on her last day, thinking that this would give her time to get home before nightfall. But she had arranged to meet Matthew at five o'clock, so she had the afternoon to waste. Mary took time packing her few things together and saying goodbye to the animals and the other farm workers, but it was still very early when she set out for their meeting place. When she got there she stowed her bag under a bramble bush and then loitered about. Time dragged. And then she had an idea. She would play a trick on Matthew. Near the stile was a huge, old tree with overhanging branches. She would climb up the tree and hide so that when Matthew came he would think she wasn't there. Then she would leap down and make him jump. She was still a child in many ways. With little trouble Mary climbed the tree and made herself comfortable in a crook of the branches.

It was still quite early and Matthew would not be coming for quite a long time so Mary was surprised to see two figures making their way across the field towards the stile.

They were too far off to see who it was but Mary remained hidden. As they came closer, Mary was surprised to see that one of them was, indeed, Matthew and the other was his 'foxy friend'. Mary had met Matthew's 'foxy friend' at the Harvest Supper as well and she didn't like him. There was something sly and untrustworthy about him, which is why she had come to think of him as his 'foxy friend'. They were both carrying something over their shoulders and when they came closer, Mary saw that Matthew had a spade and his 'foxy friend' a pickaxe. When they reached the stile they stopped and looked round and then, without a word, started to dig.

Mary, in the tree, watched with mounting horror as the hole they were digging took on the shape and size of a grave.

When they had finished, the two youths stood back and leaned on their tools and Mary dimly made out some of their conversation.

'This will surprise that silly young fool…'

'It's not what she's expecting at all…'

'To think that I'd be interested in her…'

'No, her money's much more interesting…'

'We'll knock her on the head, pop her in the hole and be gone… No one will suspect us.'

Matthew, her Matthew, planning such a horrible deed! She didn't believe it. Although she was feeling cold and cramped and faint from the horror of what she'd discovered, Mary stayed silent up the tree.

Time crept past until, at last, Matthew and his friend decided that they'd drawn a blank. She wasn't coming after all. She must have gone on ahead.

'Well, we'd better fill in the hole,' they decided. 'We don't want to arouse anyone's suspicion.'

Mary waited until Matthew and his 'foxy friend' had filled in the hole, stamped down the earth and scattered leaves over it and then disappeared out of sight across the field before she dared to climb down from the tree. Then she retrieved her bag and made her way home. It was well after dark before she arrived, but her family were so pleased to see her that no one wondered about this.

At first everything seemed well, but over the next few days Mary's parents began to feel that something wasn't right. Mary said that she was happy at the farm and she wanted to go back, but there seemed to be a weight on her mind and eventually it all burst out and she told them about what had happened with Matthew and his 'foxy friend'.

Obviously Mary's parents were angry and upset and swore all kinds of vengeance on the two rogues but, when he'd cooled down a little, Mary's father came up with a better plan.

They invited the neighbours and all Mary's friends round on Saturday evening for a 'Welcome Home' party and they sent a special invitation to Matthew and asked him to bring his friend as well 'to make up the numbers for the dancing'.

On Saturday evening they all arrived and they had a real, good, old-fashioned ceilidh: everyone did their party piece, some people sang songs, some recited poems, someone told a story and they all danced several dances to the scraping of a fiddle. After a while they stopped for something to eat and Matthew said to Mary, 'Mary, aren't you going to do something? Don't you know any songs or poems?'

Mary appeared to think for a while and then said 'Well, I do know a riddle…' Everyone was hushed and Mary said:

> One moonlit night I sat on high
> Waiting for one, but two came by;
> The boughs did bend my heart did quake
> To see the hole the fox did make.

Everyone was quiet. They all looked at each other, puzzled. Only two people in the room understood the riddle. Matthew and his 'foxy friend' quietly sneaked out of the room and ran for their lives. They knew that their secret was known.

And that's the end of the story. Matthew and his 'foxy friend' were never seen again in that neighbourhood. Mary did go back to work for the farmer and his wife for several more years until she met another young man, who turned out to be much more trustworthy than Matthew. They married and settled down to raise a family and lived happily for the rest of their lives.

DOROTHY VERNON AND JOHN MANNERS
A DERBYSHIRE ROMEO & JULIET

> The horses are waiting
> And ready am I!
> The storm is abating
> Come, love, let us fly!
> Oh grant me one moment!
> The horses are waiting
> Dear Haddon, goodbye!

Sir Arthur Sullivan

It has been said that the facts do not necessarily convey the truth of a situation and, conversely, that a true story does not have to stick absolutely to the facts. We see an overall picture of an event coloured by many other things, least of all the facts. This is true of both things that happen to us personally and to events of national importance. The elopement of Dorothy Vernon and John Manners is one of the best known tales of the Peak District. Sir Arthur Sullivan (of Gilbert and Sullivan fame) wrote an opera called *Haddon Hall*, 'the only Sullivan opera based on a known historical incident', and in 1924 Mary Pickford starred in a film about the event called *Dorothy Vernon of Haddon Hall*.

We also 'know' it is all true because when we visit the house we are shown the very door through which Dorothy slipped out onto the terrace to meet her lover, and we can walk down 'Dorothy Vernon's steps'! However, a historian might say that it is by no means certain that any of it actually happened and, if it did, then it almost certainly did not happen in the way the story says.

But I am a storyteller, not a historian, so here is the love story of Dorothy Vernon and John Manners which could well be thought of as the Derbyshire equivalent of *Romeo and Juliet*. Fittingly, it all happened just a few years before William Shakespeare was born. In it we have a young couple united by their love for each other but separated by the bitter rivalry between their two powerful families, and by their religions.

Dorothy Vernon was the younger daughter of Sir George Vernon of Haddon Hall, a powerful and important man who was proud to be known as 'the King of the Peak'. He gained this unofficial title because of the huge amount of land he held in the area. John Manners was the second son of the 1st Duke of Rutland. Sir George and the Duke of Rutland were great rivals to be thought of as the chief nobleman in the region. It was the classic rivalry between an ancient family and 'new blood', and it was made worse by the fact that the Vernons were Catholic and the Manners were Protestant. When the subject of their love arose, Sir George declared that his daughter would definitely not marry 'that beggarly younger son of a newly-created Earl, it is out of the question'.

Dorothy and John were deeply in love, however. They had known each other since childhood and always assumed that one day they would marry. They were not going to let something as trivial as their families get in the way. All they needed was the opportunity to elope. They were sure that if they did marry, their families would relent and accept the situation.

One day, Dorothy's father announced that there would be a huge hunting festival at Haddon Hall to which all the noble families in the area would be invited. It was to last for several days, with hunting for the men in the daytime followed by balls, feasts and entertainments in the evenings. Dorothy and John felt sure that an opportunity for them to run away together would arise during this time, so made their plans accordingly.

On the third evening of the festival a sumptuous party was held to which many other people from outside were invited as well, so there was a lot of coming and going. There was food and drink and dancing, and the young, beautiful Dorothy found herself the centre of attraction. Several young nobles sang ballads about her and many toasts were drunk 'to the beauty of Dorothy Vernon'. As the evening wore on the competition for her favour became more and more heated and Sir George began to fear that things might get out of hand and that disappointed young noblemen might resort to violence, so he sent her up to her chamber with her maid. This was the opportunity she needed. Some time after midnight, Dorothy suggested to her maid, Nan Malkin, that she should go out to say goodnight to her lover. Nan was thrilled at this kindness by her mistress and quickly slipped away. As soon as she was gone, Dorothy dressed and crept down the stairs and out of a small door onto a terrace where Sir John was waiting for her.

Creeping through the darkness they thought they might be discovered and betrayed when a keeper, who was pa-trolling the grounds, suddenly came upon them. Luckily, with their cloaks on and hoods up the keeper could not recognise them. The taller of these two mysterious figures called out to him, 'Jasper Jugg, is that you? Nan Malkin is whispering with her lover down below the terrace and she has left her mistress unattended. Go and tell her to get back to her duty straight away'.

John Manners knew that Jasper Jugg, the keeper, had a soft spot for Nan so the news that she was whispering with someone else sent him rushing off and out of their way at top speed. As soon as Jasper had gone, John Manners took a silver whistle from his pocket and blew it softly. From out of the trees came several armed men leading horses. The two lovers mounted and rode off into the night. When they reached John's family home in Leicestershire they were welcomed and, a few days later, married.

Sir George Vernon was understandably furious about the elopement and apoplectic with rage when he heard of the wedding, but he loved his daughter and his anger soon cooled and they were reconciled.

On Sir George Vernon's death, Sir John and Dorothy Manners inherited Haddon Hall and lived there until Dorothy died aged forty. Sir John lived out the rest of his life there but never remarried. Haddon Hall has remained the home of the Manners family to this day.

MURDER IN WINNAT'S PASS

Like several of the other tales in this book, this story features lead miners. Lead has been mined in Derbyshire since at least Roman times and its extraction has always been an important industry. The scale of it was vast. Even now you can follow the track of the underground veins for many miles across fields and hills by the pock marks and spoil heaps left on the surface. The miners dug horizontally into hillsides or vertically downwards for many yards following the ore and they often lived in houses dug into the ground. It was a hard, dangerous and unhealthy life. Daniel Defoe, in his *Tour Through the Whole Island of Great Britain*, describes a lead miner who unexpectedly emerged from the ground in front of him near Wirksworth:

> He was clothed all in leather, had a cap of the same without brims… he was as lean as a skeleton, pale as a dead corpse, his hair and beard a deep black, his flesh lank, and, as we thought, something of the colour of the lead itself… nor could we understand any of the man's discourse so as to make out a whole sentence…

It is not surprising that these people were hard and rough, a huge contrast to the gentlefolk with whom we start this story.

Henry and Clara were in love, but their parents were against the relationship. Although Henry was a gentleman, Clara was of noble birth and her parents would not have her marry beneath herself so they banned them from seeing each other. In fact, Clara's parents were in the process of arranging for her to marry someone else, someone they thought more suitable, someone nearer her own station. There was only one thing for Henry and Clara to do – elope.

They had been planning it for weeks. They couldn't meet each other because Clara, particularly, was never left alone and always had to take a chaperone when she went out, but they managed to hide letters in secret places and send messages with the help of friends or servants. On the appointed day, Henry waited at the bottom of the lane near Clara's house with two horses and a bag containing all the money he could get hold of and a few other things which he thought they might need. Soon after midday, Clara excused herself from her parents saying she had a headache and was going to lie down. Once in her room she slipped on her outdoor shoes and threw a cloak over her dress and carefully climbed out of the window onto an outhouse roof and from there down to the ground. Expecting to hear the uproar of discovery at every step, she slipped through the gate and down the lane to where Henry was waiting. Pausing only for the briefest of embraces they climbed onto the horses and rode as quickly as they dared away from the house.

When they thought they were safe from pursuit they slowed so that it wouldn't tire the horses too much. They had a long way to go. They were heading for Castleton in the Peak District because they knew that near there, in the chapel in Peak Forest, they could marry without their parent's permission. Peak Forest had once been a Royal Hunting Forest and, for some arcane reason, forest laws still prevailed there and they were different to the usual laws which were observed in the rest of the country. One of these oddities was that the vicar in the Peak Forest Chapel was allowed to perform marriages on demand. Couples didn't have to live there for weeks before or post bans, the vicar did not even have to ask their ages or where they came from. Because of this he was much in demand from couples like Henry and Clara who wanted to get married in a hurry and in secret for any one of many reasons – pregnancy, fortune, fear… The list goes on, but more often than not the reason was simple – the couple were in love and their parents would not agree to their marriage. Often the vicar would be woken in the night and have to perform the ceremony in his nightclothes so that the couple could go on their way before the pursuing family could catch up with them! Obviously he was well paid for his services!

When Henry and Clara arrived at Castleton it was late and getting dark. They went into the inn for a meal and a rest and to ask directions. Whilst in the inn a group of lead miners noticed them, and the bag Henry was carrying. They overheard them asking for directions, guessed where they were going and why, and decided, rightly, that the bag probably contained all their wealth. The miners quietly slipped out of the inn and made their way into Winnat's Pass to wait for the travellers.

Winnat's Pass is an amazing place. The land all around Castleton is full of caves and potholes and the pass was formed hundreds of thousands of years ago when the roof of a gigantic cavern collapsed. From Castleton the road climbs steeply and you enter the pass through a gateway of tall cliffs. The narrow track, as it was in those days, then winds past pillars of rock speckled with caves and you are hemmed in by sheer rock walls so there is no means of escape. The wind usually roars down the hill into your face, making progress difficult. In fact, the name Winnat's probably comes from 'windy gates'! You eventually come out at the top of the hills many hundreds of feet higher than when you started. It is an ideal place for an ambush and that is what those five lead miners planned.

When Henry and Clara reached the start of the pass they both dismounted as the horses could not carry them up the steep hill. They had gone only a little way when they found themselves surrounded by a gang of rough men who demanded the bag and all their money. It would have made no difference if they had handed them over passively or not, for the miners were not going to leave witnesses. Henry's throat was cut and Clara was beaten to death with a pickaxe handle. All their belongings were taken and their bodies were hidden in one of the myriad caves and mines which dotted the slopes.

The next day Clara's parents came to Castleton asking whether the couple had been seen and they were told that they had been in the inn and had set out for the chapel. The vicar denied having married them but Clara's parents weren't sure whether or not to believe him – he might have been trying to put them off the scent. They hunted high and low and offered rewards for finding the runaways, but to no avail. They feared the couple might be dead, or they could have been living secretly and happily anywhere in

England, or they may have taken ship to one of the colonies. No one was sure.

Many years passed before the truth came out and it was one the murderers themselves who told the story. It seems that after the murder, far from enjoying the proceeds of their deeds, nothing went right for the five miners. They weren't particularly bad men and they were overtaken with guilt and imagined that the pass was haunted by the ghosts of the murdered lovers. Eventually they all came to bad ends. One of them, John Bradshaw, was killed by a fall of stones in a mine; another, Nicholas Cock, fell from the cliffs whilst drunk and broke his neck. This seemed too much of a coincidence and it drove one of the remaining three men, called Francis Butler, mad. The fourth miner, Thomas Hall, committed suicide. The last of the robbers lived on for several more years but then made a death-bed confession and begged for forgiveness. It was he who revealed where the bodies were hidden.

All this happened in the 1750s. Laws were changed over the next few years to make such marriages more difficult and they were eventually stopped completely in 1804 when the then vicar of Peak Forest Chapel closed his special Runaway Marriages Register with the words, 'Here endeth the list of persons who came from different parishes in England and were married at Peak Forest'.

> Christians, I have told my ditty,
> If you shudder not with fear,
> If your breasts can glow with pity,
> Can you now withhold a tear?

LOVER'S LEAPS
AND OTHER SMALLER STEPS

I guess there must be places called Lover's Leap all over Britain, particularly in hilly areas or where there are cliffs. There are several in Derbyshire. Perhaps the best known is the one in Dovedale. It was named Lover's Leap about 200 years ago. A young woman heard that her lover had been killed whilst off fighting against Napoleon. She was so overcome with sorrow that she climbed to the top of the hill and threw herself off into the void below. Luckily for her, her billowing skirts caught in branches on her way down and she was able to scramble to safety. When she returned home she found that the news of her lover's death had been a mistake and he was actually on his way home to her. Lucky indeed!

There is another Lover's Leap in Ashwood Dale. Two lovers were mounted on one horse, bound for the Peak Forest Chapel to be married. They were being pursued by their parents. who were against the union and were rapidly gaining on them. When the couple found the chasm across their path they seemed to be trapped but, rather than stop and be caught, they decided to risk all and leap across. They did not really expect to succeed, particularly with two on the one horse, but they felt they would rather die together than be separated forever. Miraculously, the horse made the jump and they landed safely on the other side. Their parents, however, would not risk the jump and turned back, allowing them time to marry before being caught. By then it was too late to do anything about it.

In nearby Lathkill Dale is Jane Hambleton's Rock. At the top of this rock Jane's lover promised to marry her, but only on condition that she should jump off the rock to prove her love for him! She did so – twice – and suffered only a broken finger! But the young man was still not satisfied – or perhaps he just couldn't bring himself to marry her, so, desperately looking for a way out, he insisted that Jane should jump once more. She did and this time she was killed. So she did go up the aisle, but in a coffin, not as a bride.

The best Lover's Leap story comes from Stoney Middleton, a little place equidistant between Buxton, Matlock, Chesterfield and Sheffield.

Hannah Baddeley lived at Stoney Middleton, which is a well-named place being at the bottom of a deep limestone gorge along the bottom of which winds the one main street. Some of the houses are built into the cliffs so the inhabitants are described as troglodytes! In the shadow of those cliffs it always seems dark. Today it is very industrial, with huge quarries and stone workings and a pall of limestone dust and exhaust fumes seems to hang, permanently, over the place. In Hannah's day, though, it was much smaller and the workings were on a more human scale.

Hannah had spent her whole life in Stoney Middleton and had lived happily with her mother and father. She was a dutiful daughter and never thought about marrying or moving away. Until, that is, she was nearly twenty-five years old – quite old to still be a spinster in those times. It was then that Hannah met William Barnsley. He made an immediate impact on Hannah and she on him. It was love at first sight.

In the slow, respectful manner of the times William courted Hannah. He visited her at home with her parents present; together they visited friends or relations and, alone, they went for walks on the hills. It was assumed by everyone around that they would marry, and towards the end of the first year of this courtship William felt compelled to propose to Hannah. She was delighted and wore his ring with pride. However, William's love for Hannah had cooled after the first flush of the relationship and he found himself unable to commit himself to naming a day. Eventually he could bear it no longer and confessed to Hannah that he no longer loved her and could not marry her.

Hannah was heartbroken. She kept the news to herself but sank into a deep despair. She thought, or hoped, that it was just a hiccup, that William had got cold feet and that soon he would realise that he could not live without her as she could not live without him. She tried to talk to him to persuade him, but he avoided her.

Then one day she climbed to the top of the tall cliffs overlooking the main street. There she took off her cloak and bonnet, folded them on a stone, and leapt into the void.

There are several different versions of what happened next. She was definitely not killed outright by the fall, miraculous as that may seem. Some say that she was crippled and died after two years of pain. Some say that she was bruised and battered by the fall and that her clothes were torn by the brambles and branches she was snared on during her descent, but that she was able to get up and walk home. The third, most romantic, account says that her

petticoats and voluminous skirts opened like a parachute and lowered Hannah safely down to ground level!

Whichever of these endings is true, Hannah was cured of her love for William and she died two years later, still a spinster. In memory of the event the cliff from which Hannah jumped was renamed Lover's Leap and the inn below the cliff is now the Lover's Leap Café.

SPINNERS AND WEAVERS

In the seventeenth and eighteenth centuries whole areas of Derbyshire and Nottinghamshire were engaged in the cloth manufacturing industry. At first it continued to be done by hand as it had been since the beginning of history. The wool or cotton was spun into thread using a spindle and then it was woven into cloth on a hand loom. As time went by improvements were made to the processes, culminating in mechanisation and the birth of the factory system under Richard Arkwright at Cromford. His first water-powered mill was opened there in 1771.

Before that though, there was rivalry and jealousy between spinners and weavers. Each thought they were the most important part of the process, but the weavers couldn't weave if the spinners didn't spin, and there was no reason why the spinners should spin if there weren't any weavers for them to supply. They were interdependent. The competition was made worse by the fact that spinning was mainly done by young women (so we get the word spinster for an unmarried woman) and most weavers were men.

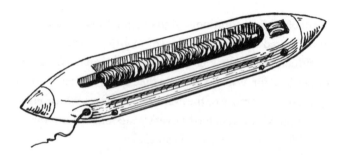

One day a young woman, who happened to be a weaver because she had inherited her father's loom, went along to the church to post the bans for her forthcoming marriage. The vicar questioned her and took down all the details he needed – her name, her age, where she lived, and so on.

And then he asked the simple question which started the trouble. 'And, of course, you're a spinster?' he said. It was mainly a rhetorical question but it gained an answer.

'No, no, I'm a weaver', she stated.

'No, that's not what I mean', said the vicar. 'You're not married already, so you are a spinster.'

'No, I'm not, I've just told you, I'm a weaver', she insisted. Deadlock.

The young woman was adamant that she was not a spinster, she was a weaver; and the vicar could not make her understand what he was asking.

After the conversation had gone round and round for what seemed an eternity the vicar, in exasperation, shouted, 'Young woman, are you ignorant?'

'Of course I am, three months, why else would I be getting married?'

THE BLINK-EYED COBBLER

All you that delight in merriment
Come listen to my song,
It is very new and certain true,
You need not tarry long,
Before you laugh your belly full
Therefore be pleased to stay,
I hope that you will be pleased,
Before you go away.

There was a rich gentleman of Derbyshire, a widower, whom we will call Sir John. Sir John lived with his son, young John, a young man in his twenties, and several servants. Young John had unfortunately – or perhaps fortunately, you can decide when you've heard the story – fallen in love with a chambermaid named Sue. Sue was a good looking, lively young woman who could easily have passed as a Lady if she had so desired. Sue loved young John in return, and kisses and fondling in corners soon moved on to young John visiting Sue in her room at night, and it was not long before, as you may guess, Sue found herself to be pregnant. Now this couple, despite their different backgrounds, really did love each other; it was not a simple case of a young gentleman taking his pleasures with an available servant girl only to discard her when things went wrong. As soon as Sue told him of her predicament, young John promised that he would marry her – and soon.

One Friday evening, thinking themselves alone in the house, young John told Sue of the plans he'd made.

'We will marry on Sunday', he said. 'I have it all arranged.'
He then went on to tell Sue the details. But young John's
father had returned home unexpectedly and, hearing voices where there shouldn't have been any, stood listening
nearby and heard everything that was said. As the conversation went on Sir John grew more and more furious. He
would not have his family name disgraced by his son marrying a servant girl, or his servant giving birth to a bastard
in his house. Saying nothing he crept up to his rooms to
ponder on the problem.

The next morning Sir John called the two young people
to him in his study. 'I understand that you two are to wed
on Sunday', he said. 'Well, you may as well put it off until
Monday or forever because it is never going to happen. I
plan to part you once and for all. Tonight!'

He then told Sue that if she kept quiet about the father
of her child he would make sure she was taken care of and
pay a small sum towards its upkeep. With that he gave Sue
her wages and sent her home. His son he confined to his
room.

The next morning, Saturday, young John was sent off
– banished – to his uncle's house in London, escorted by
a trusted servant. The plan was for him to stay there until
his father could make other arrangements for his future;
perhaps he would be sent overseas or he might be married
if a suitable match could be found. Whatever happened,
for the good of the family name, he and Sue must be kept
from one another. Although Sir John trusted the servant
who had been in his employ for decades, this man had
known young John ever since his birth and was very fond

of him, so when young John offered him 20 guineas if he would allow him to stray from their route to visit Sue at her home the servant reluctantly agreed.

Sue was delighted to see her lover – she had been afraid she had lost him forever – and he assured her that they would still marry. He had a plan and with Sue's help he started to put it into operation.

First he disguised himself a poor, blink-eyed cobbler with a red beard and a leather apron. Then he went and boldly knocked on Sir John's door. Sir John himself opened the door and the cobbler addressed him. 'Sir,' he said, 'I am aware that your son has played wanton tricks with your chambermaid who is now in an embarrassing condition. I also understand that you intend to pay a sum of money to support the child when it is born… This could be a costly exercise. You never know what tricks the maid might play and what costs could arise. Well, I am willing to take all this responsibility off your hands. For a one-off payment of £50 I will marry the girl and bring up the child as my own. Then you need worry no more about it.'

Sir John could not believe his luck, although it didn't cross his mind to wonder how the cobbler knew so much about his affairs. 'Before I part with one ha'penny,' he said, 'I will see the deed done. I will see the pair of you safely married and I will give the bride away myself! That way I will know it is all done properly.'

Straightaway they went to the church where Sue and the blink-eyed cobbler were married and Sir John happily handed over the £50. He went home with a light heart, happy to be free of the problem once and for all, while the bride and groom made their way to London where they used the money to find themselves lodgings and buy Sue some dresses fitting of her new station.

A few weeks later young John sent a letter to his father saying that he had settled in London and had met and fallen in love with a beautiful, rich, young Lady who was worth £5,000. They wanted to marry, young John said, so would his father come to meet her and give his consent.

Sir John, being very pleased with the way his plans had worked out, had his coach made ready immediately and set off to London. When his son introduced the 'rich young Lady' he was even more impressed and it did not cross his mind that this could be his ex-chambermaid dressed up in rich clothes and bedecked with rings and bangles.

As soon as he could, Sir John took his son aside and whispered, 'Leave nothing to chance. Marry her as soon as possible. Today if you can!' And so, young John and Sue were married for a second time. That evening, after dinner, his father quietly told young John how he had solved the problem at home by marrying the troublesome chambermaid to a poor blink-eyed cobbler – and it had only cost him £50!

Young John rose from his chair. 'Stay there, father', he said and went off to his room where he put on his cobbler's disguise. Then he and Sue faced his father and fell down on bended knees before him. 'Forgive me, father,' he said, 'for I was that blink-eyed cobbler and this fine Lady is your old servant, Sue!' He then explained all that had happened.

Anger, puzzlement, wonder – all the emotions possible flittered across Sir John's face. He was silent for a while and then let forth a bellow of laughter. 'It was a good trick,' he said 'and I can't be angry. I hope the pair of you are as happy as your mother and I were before she was taken from us.'

Then he called for the fiddlers and announced that they would all dance the night away in honour of the young couple.

> So here's good health to the cobbler,
> With another to handsome Sue,
> Let every one drink off his glass,
> Without any more ado.

Two

FAIRY TALES

Fairy tales don't necessarily have fairies in them but there are usually some otherworldly creatures, be they giants or ogres, talking animals or witches; and there could be magic or shape-changing and other strange occurrences. Nor are fairy tales necessarily aimed at children, although most of those here would be perfectly suitable for them.

Many of the tales in this section could perhaps be included in the 'supernatural' section – in fact, I considered merging them, but there is a difference: fairy tales are definitely seen as fiction whereas some, at least, of the supernatural tales are, or were, considered to have an element of truth about them.

KITTY GREEN

Sidney Addy collected a version of this story but I first came across it in an old encyclopaedia which I used to pore over when I was a child.

Once upon a time there was a little girl called Kitty Green. Kitty Green lived in the village of Castleton in the Hope Valley in the Peak District and was a very good little girl who always did what she was told – well, almost always. This story is about the one time when she didn't.

It was a Sunday in summer – a beautiful, hot, summer's morning with the sun shining and the birds singing and the whole valley humming with the heat. Kitty was supposed to be going to church as she did every Sunday, but it seemed a pity to shut herself up in a dim, dank building on such a morning so, for once in her life, Kitty disobeyed. She walked right past the church and up the dale onto the hills. It was beautiful up there and very quiet. She saw a few sheep and the occasional jackdaw. There were traces of rabbits, although they were all hidden away in their burrows and she did not see another soul.

Kitty walked on and on until, by chance, she came to the Sleeping Mountain. As its name suggests, if you ventured onto the Sleeping Mountain you began to feel tired and then you sat down to rest and then you fell asleep. That is what happened to Kitty.

As she was sleeping, the Giant of the Peak came upon her and picked her up and took her home to be his servant. Kitty discovered that it wasn't too bad being the giant's servant, although she missed her parents and wished she hadn't been disobedient that Sunday morning and had gone to church as she was supposed to.

One morning the giant said he was going down to the river to bathe and he took Kitty along to look after his things while he was bathing. He gave Kitty his ring and his ball and

 said whatever you do, do not put the ball in the ring! But if you have a ring and a ball there is nothing more natural than to see if the one will go in or on the other and Kitty, without thinking, slipped the ball into the ring. At the very moment she did this she happened to be wishing that she was back home with her parents. And next moment she was!

They were very pleased to see her and she told them all about her adventure and promised not to disobey them again. Over the next few weeks it did not take much experimenting to discover that she only had to put the ball into the ring and wish, and whatever she wished for happened. So Kitty and her family lived a long, happy life and never wanted for anything any more.

THE LADY WHO LIVED IN A GLASS HOUSE

This is another story from Castleton but it is related to a tale commonly found all over Europe. The Grimms called it 'The Juniper Tree' and Scottish travellers call it 'Appley and Orangey'. It is a strange tale.

In Castleton there lived a little girl who made her living by selling oranges. She would take them from door to door round the town and sell one here, and two there… One day she went to the Glass House to see if the lady who lived there would buy some oranges. The Glass House was all made of glass, not just glass windows but glass walls, glass roof, glass floors… glass everything. The lady who lived there had a reputation! She was fierce and people kept away from her, but the little girl plucked up her courage and went and knocked on the glass door.

The lady opened the door and said yes, she would like some oranges… in fact she would buy all the little girl's oranges on condition that she would come and work for her as her servant. The little girl said that she'd have to ask her mother first. So she went home and asked her mother and she said she could, so the little girl went off to be servant to the lady who lived in a Glass House.

And it was alright working in the Glass House until, one day, while she was dusting, she dropped a mirror and it broke. The mirror cracked the floor and the little girl was scared so she ran off.

She ran until she came to the gooseberry tree and said:

> Gooseberry tree, gooseberry tree, please hide me,
> Or the Old Woman will find me,
> And if she does she'll break my bones,
> And bury me under cold marble stones.

And the gooseberry tree said he couldn't help but the girl should go to the butcher's.

When she got to the butcher's she said:

> Butcher, butcher, please hide me,
> Or the Old Woman will find me,

And if she does she'll break my bones,
And bury me under cold marble stones.

The butcher said he couldn't help but the girl should go to the baker's.

When she got to the baker's she said:

Baker, baker, please hide me,
Or the Old Woman will find me,
And if she does she'll break my bones,
And bury me under cold marble stones.

The baker said he would help and he emptied out a big wooden box which he used to keep sacks of flour in, and he told the little girl to get inside. Then he nailed the lid on.

Meanwhile the lady who lived in the Glass House had discovered the broken mirror and the cracked floor and set out to find the culprit. She went to the gooseberry tree and asked if he had seen the little girl, and the tree said he hadn't but the old woman should ask the butcher.

So she went to the butcher and asked if he had seen the little girl, and the butcher said he hadn't but the old woman should ask the baker.

So she went to the baker and asked if he had seen the little girl, and the baker said he hadn't but the old woman didn't believe him and she went sniffing and snuffling around the baker's shop until she came to the big, wooden box and her nose twitched and she ordered the baker to take off the lid. When the box was opened there was the

little girl hiding inside. The old woman took her by the arm and dragged her off towards the Glass House.

Just as they were entering Castleton the pair had to cross the bridge over the river and as they were doing so the old woman stopped and looked over the bridge and the girl gave her a push and she fell in and was swept down the river and drowned.

And the little girl went singing merrily until she got to the Glass House, and she kept it as her own and lived there happily ever after.

THE SMALL-TOOTH DOG

This is the Derbyshire version of one of the most famous fairy tales of all, and one which everyone knows, 'Beauty and the Beast'.

Once upon a time there was a merchant who travelled all over the country buying and selling. He also owned a fleet of ships and sometimes travelled far and wide to strange countries in search of exotic goods to trade. When he was on one of these journeys he was attacked by bandits who carried off all his goods and money. His life was only saved thanks to a small-tooth dog which happened to come on the scene at just the right moment and frighten the bandits off.

The dog took the merchant to his house which was very grand, and he dressed the merchant's wounds and looked after him until he was fully recovered from his ordeal. When the time came for him to leave, the merchant said he would like to give the dog something as a token of his thanks and to show how grateful he was.

'Will you accept of me a fish I have which can speak twelve languages?' asked the merchant.

'No, I will not', said the dog.

'Then will you accept of me a goose which lays golden eggs?' asked the merchant.

'No, I will not', growled the dog.

'Then will you accept of me a mirror in which you can see what people are really thinking?'

'No,' said the dog, 'I will not.'

'Then what can I offer you? asked the merchant.

'I will have the thing you hold most dear', said the dog. 'Bring me your only daughter!'

When he heard this the merchant was very sorry for his daughter was, truly, the thing he held most dear.

'In that case,' said the merchant, 'give me one week after I have returned home in which to spend time with my daughter and to take my leave of her and then you may come and fetch her.'

The dog agreed and, sure enough, at the end of the week he came and knocked on the door of the merchant's house. His daughter had been told about the bargain and, although she wasn't very pleased with the idea, she was prepared to go with the dog for her father's sake. She came out of the house and climbed onto the dog's back and he ran off like the wind, back to his own house. The merchant's daughter stayed with the dog for a month and was treated very well and was quite comfortable in his grand house, but towards the end of that time she started to feel homesick and she moped around the house looking very unhappy. When the dog asked her what was the matter, she said that she wanted to go to see her father. The dog agreed that she could go, on condition that she only stay for three days.

'But before I let you go,' said the dog, 'what do you call me?'

'A great, foul, small-tooth dog', she replied. 'Then,' said the dog, 'I will not let you go.' The girl cried so much at this that the dog relented and said he would take her. 'But what do you call me?' he asked.

'Your name is "As-sweet-as-a-honey-comb"', said the girl.

'Then jump up on my back and I'll carry you home.'

When they were well on the way back to the merchant's house they came to a stile. The dog slowed. 'What do you call me?' he asked.

'A great, foul, small-tooth dog', said the girl thinking that they were nearly home. 'Then,' said the dog, 'I will not let you go', and he didn't jump over the stile but turned and ran back towards his house. They stayed at the dog's house for a full week and then girl again begged the dog to take her home.

'What do you call me?' he asked.

'Your name is "As-sweet-as-a-honey-comb"', said the girl.

'Then jump up on my back and I'll carry you home.' So the girl got on the dog's back and off they ran. When they got to the stile, the dog asked, 'What do you call me?'

'Your name is "As-sweet-as-a-honey-comb"', said the girl and on they ran until they came to a second stile. By now they were almost within sight of the merchant's house so when the dog asked, 'What do you call me?' she did not think he would turn round and take her all the way back again.

'A great, foul, small-tooth dog', she said. The dog growled and leaped in the air and turned and ran at top speed back to his house where they stayed for another full week.

After she had cried and moped around for another week she again begged the dog to take her home and he agreed. So she mounted upon his back again and off they ran. When they got to the first stile, he asked, 'What do you call me?'

'As-sweet-as-a-honey-comb', and the dog jumped over the first stile. When they got to the second stile, 'What do you call me?'

'As-sweet-as-a-honey-comb', and the dog jumped over the second stile.

When they got to the gate of the merchant's house, 'What do you call me?' And the girl started to say, 'A great, f...', but she saw the sad look which started to come over the dog's face and she felt it hesitate and start to turn, so she said, 'As-sweet-as-a-honey-comb'.

And the dog walked up to the door of the house and the girl dismounted from his back and rang the doorbell. She expected the dog to leave her and run off to his own house and come back in three days time but, to her surprise, he stood up on his hind legs and reached up and pulled off his dog's head and then he wriggled and shook and stepped out of his dog's coat and there stood the finest young nobleman the girl had ever seen.

And, as you can no doubt guess, they were soon married; and, to prove this is a fairy tale, they all lived happily ever after.

THE GREEN LADY OF ONE TREE HILL

There was once a farm somewhere near Baslow. It had been in the same family for generations and it always thrived, even when neighbouring farms went through hard times. You might think this was because it was on better than average land or that the family were exceptionally talented as farmers, but they put it down to something else. On the farm was a hill on which grew three huge trees. This hill had a strange reputation and no one went near it. It was never cultivated and animals weren't grazed on it. It was just left. Only once a year, at Midsummer, did the farmer go onto the hill and lay a bunch of flowers on the roots of each tree, usually late primroses, which, in Derbyshire, were thought to have powerful magical properties. When he had done so he'd return home as quickly as he could before it started to get dark and he'd lock the doors and breathe a sigh of relief at an unpleasant, but necessary, task accomplished for another year.

His ancestors had made this offering to the 'Green Ladies' for as long as anyone could remember and it was to the Green Ladies that they put down their success and prosperity. No one knew who the Green Ladies were, in fact no one spoke openly about them or acknowledged that they were real, but occasionally, in the security of their homes, perhaps after they'd had too much to drink and had lost their inhibitions, people would tell about being out late at night and passing by the hill. Some said they had heard strange singing and laughter coming from the hill and some said they had caught glimpses of three beautiful young women dressed in green, skipping and dancing among the trees. They hadn't loitered or stopped to listen but had hurried on, for the local people preferred not to see or hear such things.

There came a day when the old farmer died and he left the farm to be divided up between his three sons. The eldest son inherited the largest portion of the farm, over half of it; the middle son inherited the larger part of what was left; and the youngest son had just a small pocket-handkerchief-sized piece of land which happened to run alongside the hill with the three trees on it. The hill itself was on the land now owned by the eldest son. Although this seems a rather unfair way of dividing up the farm, it was in keeping with the custom of the times, and it was what they were expecting and they were all satisfied.

The two eldest boys were both modern, educated young men (at least for those days, for it was a long while ago) and they set to farming in the latest fashion. They knew about 'the rotation of crops' and letting fields lay fallow, and using manure and so on, and they followed all these doctrines and more of their own invention. What they weren't interested in were superstitions and old-wives' tales, so they had no time for laying offerings of flowers on tree roots!

The youngest son was different. Although he saw sense in some of the 'new fangled' methods his brothers were so keen on and used some of them in moderation if it seemed right, he also honoured the traditional way of doing things and kept to those when they seemed to fit.

The farming years passed and the two oldest brothers were slightly disappointed at the way their farms were going. They weren't doing badly but they weren't seeing the huge improvements they were expecting from their 'scientific' methods. They looked jealously and wonderingly at the little farm their younger brother was working. It seemed to be thriving as never before, despite his old-fashioned ideas. His tiny fields of oats and barley were ripe and healthy-looking, his garden was full of all kinds of fruit and vegetables and his cows were giving good, rich milk.

One morning the eldest brother confronted the youngest. 'Who is helping you on your farm?' he asked. 'You can't be doing all this by yourself.' But he insisted that he was.

'I saw you up on the hill last night,' the elder brother shouted, 'what were you doing up there?'

'It was Midsummer's Eve so I was placing flowers on the roots of the trees as our father taught us to do', the younger replied.

'Stuff and nonsense, you keep off that hill, it's on my land and I don't want you trespassing,' said the oldest. 'Anyway, I have to do some repairs to my barn so I think I'll cut one of those old trees down and use the timber!'

The next morning the youngest brother watched sadly as the eldest made his way up the hill with a cart and horses and several of his men. He took his axe and swung it at one of the trees. The instant the axe bit into the tree there came a cry like a woman might make if you cut into her with a sharp knife. It was a horrifying sound and the horses bolted, followed by the men. The eldest brother stood his ground though, and continued to chop into the tree. He was a skilled woodsman and had felled many trees, so he knew which way it was going to fall and as soon as it started to sway he stood well back.

I don't know what happened then, was it a sudden gust of wind? The youngest brother, watching from outside his front door, saw the tree start to topple and then hesitate and twist round, and change direction and fall right on top of the man carelessly leaning on his axe.

Later that day the middle brother came with his men and horses and cut up the tree and carried the body of his elder brother back down to his house, where he was later buried.

The middle brother assumed he could take over his elder brother's farm and did so without consulting the younger one at all, but he didn't complain, he patiently carried on farming his small farm in his own way. Several years passed and every Midsummer he laid flowers on the roots of the two remaining trees and his farm continued to prosper. The music and dancing on the hill were now less often and less lively than before, and if anyone caught a glimpse of the Green Ladies, they seemed older and more careworn but, on the whole, people avoided the hill even more, so they weren't really aware.

The big farm staggered from crisis to crisis – springs dried up, animals became sick, plants withered, hens stopped laying and yields were low. The elder of the two remaining brothers got angrier and angrier and more and more jealous of his successful younger brother. In the end he took to drink.

One day it all got too much for him and he, in turn, confronted the younger. He'd seen him up on the hill the evening before. 'Don't tell me you are still carrying out those old superstitious rituals?' he taunted. 'You can't really believe they do any good? And I've seen your cattle up on the hill!' he said (he hadn't, but it was a good excuse), 'so I'm going to chop down one of those trees and build a much stronger fence to keep them out.'

History seemed to be repeating itself as the next morning he went up the hill with his horses and men and began to chop at one of the trees. Again a heart-rending scream rent the air and men and horses fled. The man continued to chop until he could see that the tree was ready to fall. He remembered what had happened to his brother so he stood well back so that, whatever happened, he could not possibly be hit by the falling tree. The younger brother watched the tree fall safely, well away from its slayer, but he couldn't believe his eyes as the remaining tree lifted a huge bough and brought it down like a sledgehammer onto the man's head!

Later, people from the village came and took the body of the middle brother away, but the body of the tree was allowed to stay where it had fallen.

The youngest brother took over all three farms and ran them quietly and successfully and continued to take flowers to place on the roots of the one remaining tree at Midsummer. He knew that sometimes the one remaining Green Lady danced a sad, lonely dance all by herself, and sometimes he heard quiet, melancholy singing on the wind.

At length he died and, as he had never married, the farm passed to another family.

Times change and landscapes change. The nearby village grew and houses were built on the fields the younger brother had once farmed with so much skill and love. Strangers who had never heard of the Green Lady moved in, but even they sensed the mystery of the place and avoided the hill.

Even today there are not many people who will venture onto One Tree Hill, although they can't give you a rational reason why they shouldn't; and you occasionally meet an old person who remembers being told, when they were a very little child, not to go on One Tree Hill because it belongs to a Green Lady.

And the one tree still stands there, all alone, but whether or not the Green Lady still dances her lonely dance and sings her melancholy song I don't know. And I don't intend to venture up the hill at night to find out!

LITTLE BLUE EYES, TURKEY AND
THE MUSIC BOX

Fairy tales have always jumped on and off the page like naughty spirits. You can't trust them longer than you can tell them! All the well-known tales from Grimm and Perrault and so on are supposed to have come from oral sources before they were written down. Others perhaps started as literary works but soon entered the oral tradition.

I cannot remember when or where I found this story. It is one I have been telling for many years. It goes down well with older children and has good opportunities for participation. It is quite an eye-opener to get them to suggest ways of being naughty! I seem to think that I heard the story from a local source, and perhaps an oral rather than a written one. However, when I started to put this book together I discovered that it is a re-telling of a Victorian short story called 'The New Mother' by Lucy Lane Clifford. Her story tells of 'the awful fate of two innocent children who are repeatedly encouraged in naughty behaviour by a strange and charming young woman who may be an evil spirit'.

Little Blue Eyes and Turkey were a brother and sister who lived right up in the hills in the wildest part of Derbyshire. They had a mother and a father, but he was a sailor so he was away at sea most of the time and they rarely saw him. In fact, he was almost a stranger, a sort of fairy tale figure like Father Christmas, who occasionally came home bringing exotic presents from distant places; or perhaps, an ogre their mother sometimes threatened them with if they misbehaved. But they didn't misbehave very often, for Little Blue Eyes and Turkey loved their mother and were good, happy children.

Now you might be wondering why the two children had such strange names. They weren't their real names of course. They had real names but I don't know what they were. The reason the little girl was called Little Blue Eyes is quite easy to guess, but why should her brother be known as 'Turkey'? It wasn't because he gobbled his food or was fat or anything like that, it was just that he liked to wear a baggy white shirt with a red handkerchief tied round his neck. He thought it made him look like a cowboy but one day, when she was feeling spiteful, his sister had said it made him look like a turkey and the nickname stuck.

Little Blue Eyes and Turkey generally got on well together, which was a good thing because it was a wild, lonely place where they lived and there weren't any other children around. Very often they would pack themselves up a picnic and spend the whole day off around the hills by themselves. They'd build themselves dens, paddle in streams, explore caves, climb trees – do all the dangerous, exciting things which children love to do if they are given the chance. Very often they'd return home at dusk having seen nobody else the whole day.

One day they were sitting on a hill eating their lunch when they heard the sound of music. It was very faint and seemed to be coming from a long way off and they had to strain their ears to hear it but, as they listened, it gradually drew nearer and nearer. They jumped up and went to where they could see down into the dale. Coming along the road in the distance they made out a small figure. They ran down and waited and after a while, round the corner, came a little girl of about their age. She was holding something and moving her hands. They couldn't quite make out what it was she was carrying, but they were sure that it was her who was making the music. When the little girl got close they ran up and greeted her and asked what it was she had.

The little girl showed them a beautiful, polished music box. The box itself was square with a handle on the side and when the girl turned the handle out came the music. It was lovely. Even better though was the fact that on the top of the box were the carved wooden figures of a couple dancing. The man was holding the woman in his arms and as the music played they went round and round. Little Blue Eyes and Turkey asked if they could try it and the little girl let them have several turns each.

They loved the music box and asked where she had got it. They wanted one like it, they said. The girl apologised and said there wasn't another like it anywhere because her father had made it especially for her. 'Oh, could he make one for us?' they asked and she explained that he couldn't because, although he'd carved the figures and made the box, the mechanism that made the music had come from somewhere else and he didn't have another one. Little Blue Eyes and Turkey were sad and frustrated and had several more turns on the music box. They offered to swap things for it or even to buy it with their tiny bit of pocket money but the little girl said she didn't want to part with it. The pleading and begging went on and on and in the end the little girl gave in and said, 'Alright, if you really want this music box so much, I'll set you a task and we'll see if you can win it'.

Little Blue Eyes and Turkey loved competitions and riddles and their mother had told them lots of stories about heroes being set impossible tasks so they were all for this.

'What have we got to do?' they asked.

'It's easy,' said the little girl, 'go home and be naughty and then meet me here tomorrow morning and we'll see whether you deserve the prize.'

Now I've already said that Little Blue Eyes and Turkey were, on the whole, good children. They didn't get into trouble very often but they thought they could manage to be naughty now if it meant they would win the music box. So they waved goodbye to the little girl and ran off home full of ideas about what naughty things they could do.

When they got there they ran straight into the house with their muddy boots on and slammed the door behind them so hard that the whole house shook and a picture fell off the wall. Their mother came bustling out of the kitchen, 'Children, children,' she said, 'slow down, what's the matter? Is something wrong?' When she saw that there wasn't anything wrong her tone changed and she said, 'How many times have I told you about slamming doors? Look what you've done – you've broken the picture... and take those muddy boots off at once!'

Instead of saying sorry and doing what they had been told, Little Blue Eyes and Turkey stuck their tongues out and ran back out of the house laughing and thinking about the music box. But it was tea-time and they were hungry so soon they had to face their mother again. 'I don't know what's got into you', she said. 'You can go straight upstairs to bed and I don't want to hear another word from you until the morning.' (Later she relented and took them up some supper, but she was still cross.)

Early the next morning, as soon as they'd had their breakfast, Little Blue Eyes and Turkey were off over the hills to the road to wait for the little girl. Time dragged by but at last they heard the sound of the music box and saw the little girl strolling along the road. They ran up to her. 'We did it! We did it!' they shouted. 'We were naughty. Can we have the music box now?'

'First you've got to tell me what you did', she answered.

'Well,' said Little Blue Eyes, 'we ran into the house with our muddy boots on and we slammed the door so hard that the whole house shook!'

'And a picture fell off the wall and smashed!' butted in Turkey. The little girl was not looking too impressed.

'And then,' they said triumphantly, 'when Mother told us off we stuck our tongues out and ran away!'

The little girl thought for a moment. 'That was quite naughty,' she said 'but nowhere near naughty enough. I'll give you another chance. Go home and be much naughtier and meet me here again tomorrow and then we'll see if you deserve the music box.'

So Little Blue Eyes and Turkey went home and this time they didn't run in but stayed outside and threw stones and clods of earth at the door. When their mother opened the door to see what was happening, they ran away. When tea-time came, Little Blue Eyes and Turkey didn't eat their food up nicely as they usually did, they played around with it and built castles of mashed potato and then started flicking it at each other and that developed into a full scale food fight, which culminated in Turkey throwing his plate at his mother!

She was both angry and sad at the way the children were behaving. She did not understand it at all. 'I wish your father would come home', she said. 'He would soon sort you out!'

Again Little Blue Eyes and Turkey were sent to bed in disgrace but they were up and full of beans in the morning and off over the hills to wait for the little girl with the music box.

As it had the morning before the wait to hear the little girl's music growing louder as she came along the road seemed like an eternity, but eventually she was there.

'We did it! We did it!' they cried. 'We've definitely won the music box this time!' and they told the little girl what they had done. 'We threw stones and mud at the door and when Mother came we ran away. Then we played with our food and built castles with the mashed potato and we flicked it at each other and Turkey threw his whole plate at Mother!' said Little Blue Eyes. The little girl looked pleased and said that they were learning, they'd soon be naughty enough to win the music box. She said they could have one more chance.

So Little Blue Eyes and Turkey ran home and into the front parlour, which they were only allowed in on Sundays, and they opened their mother's china cupboard and pulled all the best china out onto the floor (one or two items got broken). Then they went to the bookcase and tumbled the books out. While they were doing this their mother came in and was so shocked to see her good little children behaving in such a strange fashion that she stood there too stunned to say a word. Little Blue Eyes and Turkey ran out of the room slamming the door behind them, grabbed the key from off the peg in the hall where it was kept and locked their poor mother in the ransacked room.

'You children will be the death of me!' she shouted. 'What on earth has got into you? I think the fairies have swapped you! If you don't change your ways immediately you'll find yourself with a new mother and she'll have one glass eye and a wooden tail!'

Little Blue Eyes and Turkey were upset by this. They wondered whether they had gone too far this time. They didn't want a new mother, they loved the one they had, and they definitely didn't want a new mother with one glass eye and a wooden tail!

Feeling rather guilty and apprehensive, but also excited at the thought of what would happen tomorrow, they made their way to bed. In the morning they were out and off as soon as it became light. They made their way to the usual meeting place and waited for the little girl with the music box. They were certain that they had been bad enough to win it this time and they were looking forward to taking it back to show their mother and to make up with her.

They waited and waited but heard no music. Then, at last, Turkey spied a small figure coming along the road, but she looked different to she had on previous days and there was no music. When she got close they saw that she wasn't playing the music box. They ran to her and all the words tumbled out about how naughty they had been and how she just had to give them the music box this time. When she had quietened them and they had told the girl just what had happened the evening before, she thought for a minute and said, 'Ye-e-e-s, that was pretty bad. I think you deserve the music box this time... but I haven't got it!'

Little Blue Eyes and Turkey couldn't believe what they were hearing. Then the girl explained. 'We are a gypsy family,' she said, 'and we've been camping in the wood round that bend. Today we are moving. We are going off to Newark. I didn't know and Dad has packed up the caravan and he's put the music box away somewhere and I can't find it. So although you've won the prize, I can't give it to you. I'm sorry.'

Little Blue Eyes and Turkey were amazed and sad and angry... all kinds of feelings mixed up together. They said goodbye to the little gypsy girl and she went back to her parents. They stamped up onto the hills and spent the day getting rid of their disappointment by breaking down dens they had built before, throwing stones at trees, chasing crows, anything they could think of to vent their frustration.

Towards evening they thought it was time to go and face their mother, to say sorry and try to explain why they'd been behaving so badly. They were sure she would forgive them. As they reached the top of the rise and looked down on their house nestling in the dale the sun was setting behind them and one last ray of sunlight shone out through the clouds, over their shoulders, towards the house and reflected back – just as if it was reflecting off a glass eye.

And as they neared the house they heard a 'Thump! Thump! Thump!' Just the kind of thump that would be made if a wooden tail was beating on the floor!

THE LITTLE RED HAIRY MAN

This relation of 'the Golden Goose' is one of the best-known local tales amongst Derbyshire storytellers. A few years ago there were a series of story walks, each led by a different teller in different parts of the county. It became a standing joke that whoever the teller was and wherever the walk went there would be a version of the Little Red Hairy Man!

But it's a good story so it could stand repetition. This is my version.

> In come six jolly miners
> We are not worth a pin,
> We've only come a-miming
> To get a piece of tin,
> We've travelled all of England,
> Scotland, Ireland round
> And all of our delight is
> In working underground.

'Six Jolly Miners', a traditional song.

As far back as anyone can remember, one of the most important occupations in Derbyshire has been lead mining, so it isn't surprising that lead mines and lead miners feature in Derbyshire stories. The lead miner in this story lived at Youlgrave, although some tellers place him elsewhere. He had three sons. Like most lead miners the family was poor and the three sons often dreamed of finding their fortunes so that they would not have to spend their lives burrowing down into the ground, following the seams of lead.

One day the eldest son packed up a few belongings in a knapsack with some food and a bottle of drink and set off to try to change his luck. He walked at a good pace all morning and when midday came he thought he would sit down and eat his 'snap', as he called it. By the side of the road he found a big rock and thought that would make an ideal seat. As soon as he was settled and had opened his bag, a little red hairy man appeared by his feet and asked if he could share his food and drink. This little man was only a 1½ft high and had a long beard and a pointy hat on his head. He looked for all the world like a gnome or leprechaun (but he was in the wrong country to be one of those!).

Instead of sharing his 'snap' the young man kicked out at the little red hairy man and told him to be off and leave him alone. So the little man disappeared back to whence he had come. The young man ate his food and then went on his way; but he didn't find his fortune and after a few weeks he was forced to return home no better off than he had been when he had left.

Seeing this, the middle son decided he would give it a try as well – and he was certain he would do better than his brother. So he packed his small bag and took some food and drink, said his goodbyes and off he went down the same road. When midday came he sat down on the same stone that his brother had sat on and opened his bag and started to eat his dinner. Again the little red hairy man appeared and begged for some food and drink. This young man was not quite as selfish as his older brother so, when he had finished eating, he threw the little red hairy man some crumbs of cheese and the crusts off his bread and he let him drink the last few drops of water from his bottle.

The little red hairy man thanked him and said that if he wanted to find his fortune, he should go into the centre of the nearby wood. There he would find an old mine, he said, and there he would find what he was looking for. The young man wasn't very hopeful about this but thought it was worth a look so he went into the wood and found his way into the centre where, sure enough, there was an old mine. When he saw it though, he decided it was only an old, worked-out lead mine and there wouldn't be anything there worth having, and anyway, he was trying to escape from being a miner… so he went on his way.

Like his older brother he didn't find his fortune and was forced to return home after a few weeks, no better off than he had been when he had left.

Of course, seeing his two brothers come home with their tails between their legs made the youngest brother, whose name was Jack, determined to outdo them. Jack said that he would go off to seek his fortune too, and he would be successful! His older brothers laughed at him and said that if they couldn't do it then he certainly wouldn't, but the more they tried to put him off the more he wanted to go.

One morning Jack packed his bag, took some food and drink, said his goodbyes and went off down the same road that his brothers had travelled. When midday came he sat down on the same stone that his brothers had sat on and opened his bag and took out his food. Again the little red hairy man appeared and begged for some food and drink. Jack had always been a much more friendly, helpful person than his two brothers – you have to be when you're the youngest – so he said 'Of course', and broke his bread and cheese in two and gave the biggest half to the little red hairy man who gobbled it up as if he was starving. Then Jack gave the little red hairy man half of his drink too. When they had finished eating and drinking, the little red hairy man jumped up and told Jack about the old abandoned mine in the centre of the forest. 'That's where you'll find your fortune', he said, 'I'll meet you there!' and he rushed off down the track.

Jack followed on more slowly and found the little red hairy man standing by the mine. There was a large opening in the ground and over it the remains of a winch and pulleys. On the ground nearby was a mildewed basket. 'Get into the basket and I'll lower you down', said the little red hairy man. Without any hesitation, Jack got into the basket and the little red hairy man lowered him down. Down and down he went into the bowels of the earth. Then it got light and the basket landed with a bump. There standing beside the basket was the little red hairy man (or if it wasn't, it was his brother!). Stretching out in front of them was a gentle landscape of rolling hills dotted with woods and fields. The sky was blue with fluffy white clouds and the sun was shining.

'Follow the copper ball!' cried the little red hairy man and he drew out a ball made of copper and threw it as hard as he could. Down the road it ran, up hill and down dale, until it came to rest against the walls of a huge copper-coloured castle. Jack walked round the castle until he came to the gates. He banged on the copper gates and out came a giant, all clad in copper armour. Jack and the giant fought, but copper is not very good for armour and weapons so Jack was able to defeat the giant quite easily. Then he went into the copper castle and found room after room filled with treasures of every kind – gold, silver and copper coins, jewels and cloths of rich silks and brocades. Then, in the dungeon, Jack found a beautiful princess locked in a cell. He opened the door, but before he could say anything she ran off to return to her parents.

Jack started to pack the treasure into his bag but the little red hairy man called him and said, 'Leave that, follow the silver ball', and he drew out a ball made of silver and threw it as hard as he could. Down the road it ran, up hill and down dale, until it came to rest against the walls of a huge silver-coloured castle. Jack walked round the castle until he came to the gates. He banged on the silver gates and out came a giant all clad in silver armour. Jack and the giant fought. Silver is better than copper for armour and weapons and the fight was much harder than with the copper giant but, in the end, Jack was able to defeat the giant. Then he went into the silver castle and found room after room filled with treasures of every kind – gold, silver and copper coins, jewels and cloths of rich silks and brocades, all kinds of perfumes and scents, and sweetmeats of every sort. In the dungeon, Jack found a beautiful princess locked in a cell. He opened the door and she paused to thank him, but before he could say anything she ran off to return to her parents.

Jack started to pack the treasure into his bag but the little red hairy man called him and said, 'Leave that, follow the golden ball', and he drew out a ball made of gold and threw it as hard as he could. Down the road it ran, up hill and down dale, until it came to rest against the walls of a huge golden-coloured castle. Jack walked round the castle until he came to the gates. He banged on the golden gates and out came a giant all clad in golden armour. Jack and the giant fought. Now gold is better than both copper and silver for armour and weapons and the fight was much harder than it had been the previous two times. In fact, for a time, Jack thought that he might not come out on top but eventually, with a clever feint and a twist of the wrist, he was able to stab the golden giant between the visor and the breast plate and he fell down dead.

Then Jack went into the golden castle and found room after room filled with treasures of every kind – gold, silver and copper coins, jewels and cloths of rich silks and brocades, all kinds of perfumes and scents, and sweetmeats of every sort. There were chests with coronets and tiaras, necklaces and rings, stone jars filled with all the spices of Arabia and tiny boxes of sandalwood and cedar from Lebanon. In the dungeon, Jack found a beautiful princess locked in a cell. He opened the door and she came and took him in her arms and thanked him in the way that only beautiful

maidens can. Jack asked her to go home with him and marry him and she said she would be pleased to.

Jack started to pack the treasure into his bag but the little red hairy man called him and said, 'Leave that, use this one instead', and he threw Jack a small sack. As Jack shovelled the treasure into the sack his amazement grew, for it was one of those sacks he had heard of in stories – the more he put in it the more room there seemed to be and it easily held all the treasure of the golden castle.

Then, with the sack over his shoulder and the princess on his arm, Jack set out for home. His parents were pleased to see him and even more pleased when he introduced the princess who was to be his wife and emptied out the sack.

Jack and the princess and Jack's family settled down to live happily ever after. But his two brothers could not quite believe that Jack, their little brother, had succeeded where they couldn't. They quizzed him and tried to discover where the treasure had come from and even tried to retrace their steps to see where they had gone wrong.

But, of course, they hadn't been kind to the little red hairy man so he wasn't there to help them and the old, disused mine remained just that to them, and they had to live with their disappointment.

So the moral of this story is: if you are ever in Derbyshire and a little red hairy man asks you for a bite to eat, be generous and share your food with him, just in case!

Three

Tales of the Supernatural

What's the difference between fairy tales and supernatural tales? The way I have divided them is this: the fairy tales are overtly tales – fiction – and no one expects you to believe them. They are for your enjoyment only. The supernatural tales are presented as being fact. You are supposed to believe that there really is a land in the centre of the earth – if you can find the portal; the Scotsman really did travel to London thanks to witchcraft; and so on…

THE STORY OF THE DEVIL'S ARSE

This must be one of the oldest stories in this collection. It was first written down by a monk called Gervase of Tilbury in the thirteenth century and who knows for how long it had been circulating orally before that. The setting is the huge cavern near the village of Castleton which, until recently, was officially known as Peak Cavern. Now though, in order to attract tourists, it has reverted to its former, more picturesque, name of the Devil's Arse. It is odd how names change with the times; polite, scholarly Victorian travellers coyly referred to it as Arx Diabolo or Anus Plutonis thinking that, in that way, the rude, unlettered classes would not understand, but they would probably not have read their writings anyway!

There are several reasons why this cave was called by that name: first and foremost it is a very large hole! Also, on occasion, stinking winds are supposed to blow from the cave mouth and sometimes it emits floods of water – there is always a stream running from the mouth.

There are many stories from different times and places all over the world which mention entrances into the underworld, from the Greek 'Orpheus and Eurydice' to Jules Verne's *Journey to the Centre of the Earth*. Another Derbyshire entrance was believed to be the Eldon Hole.

One day the swineherd of William Peverel, the Lord of Peak Castle, which sits on the hill above the cave and overlooking the Hope Valley, lost a very valuable, pregnant sow. He had been supervising the pigs as they foraged over the hills and it was only when he returned them to their sties that he discovered the loss. He dared not let the lord know of the missing sow so he retraced his footsteps and searched every inch of the hills and dales over which the pigs had wandered that day. To no avail. He could think of nowhere else to look except in the gloom of the Devil's Arse. Perhaps it had wandered in there looking for somewhere to drop its piglets.

The huge cavern had a bad reputation and no one ventured into it except, perhaps, to shelter in the entrance but, armed with a torch, the swineherd made his way through the wide archway, across the stream that flowed across his path, and explored every nook and cranny of the cave. But there was no sign of the pig.

He daren't give up and go back empty handed though – he well knew of the cruel punishments his lord could mete out to people who let him down, so he waded through a water-filled tunnel into the next cave and on, down and down, through passageway after passageway. Sometimes they were dead-ends and he had to retrace his steps; sometimes he scrambled up or down banks of scree or clambered over boulders. By now he wasn't really thinking about the sow, he was taken up with the thrill of exploring an underground world where no one else had trodden before.

At last he thought he really should turn back, but he went on just a bit further – just round the next bend, and then the next... and just as he had finally made up his mind to turn back, he saw a glimmer of light ahead. He doused his torch and made his way towards it and the glimmer grew into a glare and he squeezed his way out of a hole halfway up a hillside into bright sunshine.

Now that was odd, for he had left the hill near Castleton as dusk was falling on a dreary, autumn evening and the view before him seemed bathed in the brilliant sunshine of midday and midsummer. It looked a world away from the poor soils and windswept hills of Derbyshire. Spread before him was a fertile valley with happy-looking peasants working in fields of golden wheat. There were orchards, the trees were laden with ripe fruit and there was a road

lined with fields of luxuriant vegetables which led to a village of neat houses. A gentle breeze soughed through the leaves, and birds sang everywhere.

As the swineherd climbed out of his hillside hole he saw, in the undergrowth just below him, the sow he had been searching for. It had farrowed and was contentedly suckling thirteen young piglets.

He would have loved to stay and explore that strange, almost Mediterranean-looking, countryside. The soil was rich and fertile, the crops were luxuriant and the sun was warm. The houses he could see in the distance looked comfortable and well cared for. The workers in the fields looked well fed and healthy. He could hear the odd burst of giggling and laughter as they shouted to each other. Snatches of song wafted across the fields. The women working nearby were curvy and attractive. He could be very happy here, he thought.

But duty called. He roused the sow and drove it and its litter back through the cave and, somehow, found his way through the labyrinth and out into the Derbyshire night where the stars blinked in a clear, chill sky and an icy wind cut through his clothes. He managed to get the sow back into its sty before it was missed and, the next day, his master rewarded him for a good litter of piglets.

After that, the swineherd's life continued much as it had always done, but he often thought of that glorious, golden land he had glimpsed down through the Devil's Arse. He wondered what would have happened if he had stayed. What opportunities would he have had? Would it really have been as idyllic as it had seemed? A few times he tried to retrace his footsteps but he never again managed to find a way through. He always came up against dead-ends or flooded passageways or found himself wandering round in circles so that, when he did see the outside world blinking through a cave mouth it turned out to be the same old Derbyshire countryside, not that other worldly Eden in the centre of the earth.

Later he told his son about it. He also searched but, as far as I know, nobody has ever found the way. But it must be there somewhere... mustn't it?

THE DERBYSHIRE WEREWOLF

North-west of Glossop in the area called Longdendale runs the Monk's Road, which was built by the monks of Basingwerk to travel between that town and their abbey near Holywell in North Wales. Along that road is a large stone called the Abbot's Chair, on which the Abbot of Basingwerk sometimes sat to hold court – to hear the complaints of his people, to dispense justice and to collect tithes and rents.

Long ago, in the reign of King Henry II, the abbot was doing just that. Towards the middle of the day there came before him a poor old woman. She was supporting herself on a stick and sobbing and was almost unable to walk with misery. She told the abbot that she had an enemy who was making her life unbearable and she had no idea what she'd done to deserve it. Through witchcraft this woman – this enemy – had already brought about the death of the old woman's husband and her children. Her cattle had all died, her crops had failed and now she had no way of supporting herself. She was penniless, had no way of feeding herself and feared that she too would soon be dead.

When the abbot asked whether there was any way for other authorities to catch and punish this woman, she told him that the witch had the power of changing shape – of appearing as either a woman or a man, or of becoming any animal or bird she wished, so it was impossible to catch her or to prove that it was she who had done any deed.

On hearing this, the abbot was furious. First he helped the old woman in a practical way by giving her a sum of money to enable her to pay her rent and feed herself for the near future and then he turned his thoughts towards the witch. He spoke a dreadful curse, 'May the hand of Heaven fall upon this wicked mortal and in whatever shape she be at the present moment, may that shape cling to her until justice be done'.

Now, that morning the old witch had changed herself into a wolf and in that shape had slaughtered several sheep in neighbouring villages. At the moment the abbot proclaimed his curse, still in wolf shape, she was sleeping off her dinner of prime mutton under a bramble bush.

By coincidence, Good King Henry himself was also in the Longdendale Forests. As the guest of the Baron of Ashton-Under-Lyne, he was indulging himself hunting in the company of other local noblemen; his son, Prince Henry; and the Lord of Longdendale. The hunting was good as the forests around there were full of deer and boasted some of the largest wild boar in the country, as well as wolves and all kinds of smaller game. The Lord of Longdendale had made the most prestigious kill so far that day, bagging several ferocious wild cats which they called 'British tigers'. The young, proud Prince Henry was eager to outdo him so he slipped off, unaccompanied, into a remote part of the forest away from the din of the hunting party where, he hoped, he could find some worthy prey. And he was not disappointed.

Prince Henry was suddenly set upon by a ferocious wolf. It charged from the undergrowth in a furious attack and the surprise and the speed of the onslaught nearly dismounted the prince. Luckily his horse took evasive action and enabled the prince to stab at the beast with his hunting spear. He felt the point enter the wolf's side and, as it did so, the beast emitted an almost human cry. Then the wolf rose up on its hind legs, took the spear in its forepaws and with its jaws snapped it in half as if it was a twig. The prince drew his sword but the beast leapt at him and knocked him from his horse before he was able to use it. They grappled on the ground, the wolf trying for the prince's throat and the prince attempting to strangle the wolf. Over and over they thrashed around and the prince's strength was rapidly fading. His life was saved in the nick of time by the Baron of Ashton, who appeared on the scene having been sent to find him when he was missed from the main party. The baron, coming up from behind, slew the wolf and rescued the prince.

Then the baron escorted the prince back to the main party and they all returned to the baron's castle. The carcass of the wolf was also taken there, along with the other game they had killed that day. After dinner, King Henry rewarded the

baron for saving the life of his son and then, with great ceremony, the huge wolf carcass was slit open and out of its stomach rolled the heads of three young children whom it had taken as a tasty snack before finding the sheep. Everyone was amazed at this as wolves rarely attack people, preferring to slink around the outskirts of their farms taking far easier prey in the shape of young or injured livestock. Everyone remarked on how unusual this wolf was and the prince spoke about its amazing ferocity and bravery. He also told of how its cries had often sounded almost human in tone.

Then a forester spoke up and said that he had a story to tell which might cast light on the mystery. Around midday, he said, he had been hiding in ambush in the forest, hoping to catch a gang of poachers who were ignoring the forest laws and taking game for their own tables, when he was startled by a thrashing in some nearby bushes. Out of them came a large wolf that seemed to be trying to scramble out of its own skin, in much the same way as a man scrambles out of his clothes. The wolf was making sounds which almost sounded like the enraged cries of an old woman. It was very unusual behaviour for a wolf, said the forester. He had seen hundreds of wolves, but had never seen or heard one like that.

While the forester was telling his tale, the Abbot of Basingwerk arrived to pay homage to the King and when he heard the story he was able to tell of his encounter that morning with the poor old woman and of his curse on the witch.

And so it became clear that the wolf killed by the Baron of Ashton-Under-Lyne was the old witch, trapped in her werewolf shape by the abbot's curse. Justice had been done far more quickly than he could ever have imagined.

And that was, officially, the last time a werewolf was seen in Derbyshire, but it is possible they are still around. You might remember that back in the 1980s, two young American tourists were attacked by one just across the border in Yorkshire. One young man died and the other, having been infected, fled to London where he wreaked havoc before being killed in wolf form. It is easy to hide on the open moors and to travel across them between Derbyshire, Yorkshire and Lancashire, so who is to say they are not still haunting the more remote spots? Every now and again farmers curse people who let their dogs worry sheep and walkers regularly report sightings of strange animals usually described as pumas or leopards. Might it not be that these things are werewolves?

THE BAKEWELL WITCHES

During the reign of James the First, the witches of Bakewell were hanged.

Edward Brooke, Attorney of the Borough Court.

About 400 years ago a Scotsman was passing through the little town of Bakewell. Although he wasn't a cattle drover he was in a related business and he had been following the old drove road all the way down from Scotland. He was travelling on foot so it had taken him several weeks so far.

When he reached Bakewell, he took lodgings at a house owned by a Mrs Stafford, a milliner who supplemented her income by taking in lodgers and putting up travellers passing through the town.

The Scotsman, pleased to have a good bed for the first time in several nights, fell fast asleep but, in the early hours of the morning, he was woken by noises from somewhere in the house and he became aware of an unusually bright light shining up through the cracks between the floor boards. He quietly got out of bed and peered through one of these cracks. In the room below, which was the kitchen, he saw his landlady, Mrs Stafford, and another woman putting on their outdoor clothes and packing luggage as if they were going on a long journey. When they were ready, Mrs Stafford chanted:

> Over thick, over thin
> Now Devil to the cellar in London.

The two women immediately vanished and the bright light faded away.

The Scotsman was startled by these strange events and repeated the words as nearly as he could remember them.

> Through thick, through thin
> Now Devil to the cellar in London.

Not quite the same but obviously close enough, for he'd hardly spoken the last word when there was a huge gust of wind which picked him up and out of the room and through the night. For several seconds he seemed to be

flying through the darkness and then it grew light and he found himself, still in his nightshirt, in a cellar and, as the two women were there, he assumed he must be in London. The two women were tying up bundles of silks and chiffons and other expensive materials which, he guessed, they must have stolen.

After this strange experience and the unexpected journey, the Scotsman was quaking with fear and seemed likely to die of shock, so Mrs Stafford gave him a cup of wine to calm his nerves. It worked so well that he fell fast asleep.

After what seemed to him like the blink of an eye, but was actually a few hours, he was awoken by a hammering at the door. He was alone in the room so he cautiously opened the door to find a watchman, who demanded to know who he was and what he was doing there in his nightshirt. The Scotsman tried to explain, but he knew that his story was unbelievable so he tried to change it and tell a more likely story. But the more he said, the more suspicious the watchman became. In the end, he put the Scotsman in chains and led him to the magistrate.

'Where are your clothes?' demanded the magistrate.

'In Mrs Stafford's house in Bakewell,' replied the Scotsman.

'So how did you come to London in your nightshirt?'

'I flew through the air!'

Now you might expect that those answers would be greeted with ridicule and disbelief, but in those days many people absolutely believed in witchcraft and were always on the lookout for any possible manifestations of it. The magistrate was one such person. He made the Scotsman tell the whole story through several times, slowly and carefully, and when he had heard it he sent a message by the speediest horse to his fellow magistrates in Bakewell saying that Mrs Stafford and her companion should be arrested immediately and tried for witchcraft on the evidence given by the Scotsman.

And that is what happened. The women had, of course, arrived back in Bakewell in no time at all and when the magistrates arrived at the house they found the packages of material which seemed to prove the story. The two women were arrested and taken to Derby Gaol. The Scotsman was taken back to Derby to give evidence. The women were tried and found guilty and were publicly executed outside the gaol in 1608, just two of many hundreds of poor women to suffer that fate.

So was the Scotsman's story true? Were they really witches and did they fly back and forth between Bakewell and London plying a trade in stolen goods? Did the Scotsman have some kind of grudge against Mrs Stafford? Or was he just trying to avoid paying his lodgings bill?

We will never know.

STRANGE GOINGS-ON AROUND CHESTERFIELD

For many, many years there have been strange goings-on around Chesterfield. Amongst other things, the town seems to have had frequent visits from the Devil. You can draw your own conclusions as to why that might be; I can't decide whether it is because the people were particularly bad and he felt at home there, or if they were particularly good and he was trying to corrupt them.

People tend to know Chesterfield for one thing above all else, and that is the crooked spire on the Church of Our Lady & All Saints. It is so well known that it has become the town's emblem. Engineers and architects will tell you that the spire is crooked because it was built of green, unseasoned timber which gradually twisted under the weight of the slates, but there are much more interesting reasons given by the folk who really know!

As I have already said, the Devil paid frequent visits to Chesterfield and on one of those occasions a local blacksmith managed to put horseshoes onto his feet – why, and how he managed it, I'm not sure, but it caused him so much pain that, in a temper, he kicked out at the spire as he flew past and knocked it out of true.

Another story says that the Devil – or Satan, or Lucifer, or whatever name he was calling himself at the time – was sitting on the spire taking a rest when the smell of incense drifted up from inside the church and made him sneeze. This caused the spire to twist.

The story to explain the crooked spire which I like best though does not concern the Devil – just the opposite. Once upon a time, and a very long time ago it was, a pure, innocent young couple came to be married in the church. The spire had been sitting there for centuries watching the world pass by and becoming quite bored by it. It thought it had seen everything and was immune to wonder by now – but it was so amazed by the purity of this couple that it turned to look at them, and stuck. It couldn't twist itself back again.

It is said that the next time a virgin gets married in Chesterfield Church the spire will stand up straight, but we may have a long wait!

As well as the Devil, Chesterfield has been threatened by other evil beasts. One of these was the Dun Cow. It had once been an ordinary cow, but a spell had been cast upon it by a local witch and it then rampaged around the countryside causing havoc. The good folks of Chesterfield needed a hero to save them and the one they chose was Sir Guy, the Earl of Warwick. Sir Guy was already a famous fighter. He had taken part in a Crusade to the Holy Land and had previously killed a green dragon and a ferocious bear, so a cow was no problem – even a bewitched one. He was able to kill the Dun Cow with one skilful thrust of his

sword. Its bones were then distributed throughout the land as proof that the deed had been done and one of its rib bones can still be seen on a tomb in Chesterfield Church.

On another occasion, a dragon flew down from the north laying waste to all the countryside in its path. A brave priest attempted to stop the dragon by climbing to the top of Winlatter Rock, which is on the moors near Chesterfield, and spreading his arms in the form of a cross. The dragon could not pass this holy sign so it summoned up great winds and storms to lash the holy man and blow him from the rock. But the priest refused to move. He stood there so long and so firmly that his feet sank into the rock and left an impression there which can still be seen to this day. Years later the dragon, perhaps guessing that the priest was dead, came back and once more started spreading destruction around the area.

Three brothers took a huge iron bar to the blacksmith and asked him to forge it into a sword.

'You won't be able to lift it', the blacksmith said.

'One can't, but three can', the brothers replied. When it was ready, the three brothers took it on their shoulders and staggered along the road to the moors. A farmer asked where they were going and when they told him, he said, 'You'll never carry that all the way to Winlatter Rock'.

'One can't, but three can', the brothers replied.

A shepherd saw them struggling up the track to the rock. 'You won't get that sword up there', he said.

'One can't, but three can', the brothers replied again.

When they reached the summit of the rock, one brother rested the sword in the priest's footprint while another ran back to Chesterfield to call out all the local men to come with their swords to help. The third brother went to the church to keep lookout and to ring the bell to sound the warning when the dragon appeared.

After a few hours the dragon arrived, flying through the evening sky like a fiery airship, destroying buildings, woods and crops as it passed. It blew a huge plume of flame towards the gigantic sword which glowed red hot like a beacon. The men of Chesterfield who were gathered round the rock held up their swords like a forest of crosses and they reflected the light back at the dragon. The dragon turned tail and sought out darkness and safety down in the depths of the Blue John Mines, near Castleton, where he remains to this day, waiting until it is safe to attack Chesterfield again.

CROOKER

If you know the road that runs from Holloway and Lea towards Cromford, you'll know that it is a narrow, lonely road with a bank rising up on one side and the River Derwent, or Darrand as it is called locally, running along on the other. In summer it can be a beautiful place to walk (if you don't mind dodging the cars, because it's a narrow road!) but in winter, when the river is running high, it can feel bleak and dangerous. Years ago there used to be a chapel on the bridge at Cromford where travellers could offer up a prayer before setting out along that road, or pause to give thanks at having arrived safely in Cromford if they were coming the other way.

That stretch of river can be very dangerous; it flows fast, there are rapids and deep pools and eddies and it can flood very quickly. It is also haunted by Crooker. Crooker has appeared at various times over the centuries with long periods of peace in between, and nobody can predict when the next spate of 'Crooker incidents' will happen. But they know when they have started, for travellers disappear and their mutilated bodies are found a few days later washed up on the banks of the river way down stream.

Because Crooker has haunted the river for so long he has attacked many travellers and there are many different versions of this story told by many different storytellers. The traveller in this version lived at the end of the eighteenth century, when Richard Arkwright had built his first mill at Cromford and when there was the threat that it might be attacked by the machine-breakers known as Luddites.

The traveller was coming from Nottingham with an important message for Cromford Mill. He had reached the tiny village of Holloway on a stormy winter's night and was battling on through the wind and rain despite warnings that he should not. When he reached Lea, the villagers came out in force and implored him not to continue. 'You should not go along that road on a night like this,' they said, 'for fear of Crooker.' Not being a local, the traveller knew nothing of Crooker, but he did know that his message was important and the sooner he reached Cromford with it the better, so he ignored their warnings, and refused their offers of accommodation, and continued on his journey.

He was not far out of Lea when a figure suddenly rose up in the road in front of him. It was an old woman dressed all in green, the colour of fairies and witches. 'Do not go along this road tonight,' she said, 'for fear of Crooker!' When the traveller started to argue she said, 'Once, years ago, you did me a favour so I am now trying to do you a favour in return. Do you remember freeing a hare from a trap? Well, I was that hare. Look, I still have the lame foot', and she lifted her skirt and showed him a deformed leg. 'Do not make this journey tonight, I warn you.' But the man insisted that he had to continue. 'In that case,' said the witch, 'if you should meet Crooker, give him these', and, although it was the middle of winter, she took from under her cloak a bunch of freshly cut primroses. The man put the flowers in his great-coat pocket, thanked the woman, and struggled on his way.

The rain lashed down, the wind howled, the trees were thrashing about over his head and his mind was full of Crooker. Suddenly another figure appeared in his path. It was another old woman dressed in green. 'Do not go along this road tonight,' she said, 'for fear of Crooker! Many years ago you rescued a raven with a broken wing. He was my companion, so now I am helping you in return. Do not travel this road tonight, I implore you.' Again, the man insisted that he must. 'In that case,' said the witch, 'if you should meet Crooker, give him these', and, she took from under her cloak a bunch of bluebells, just coming into bloom with the dew still on them. The man put the flowers in his greatcoat pocket with the primroses, thanked the woman, and went on his way.

By now he was having to lean into the wind and could barely see a few feet ahead. His eyes played tricks on him and every shape in the darkness was dangerous. Then a shadow solidified and moved out in front of him. It was a third old woman dressed all in green. 'Do not go along this road tonight,' she said, 'for fear of Crooker! Turn round and return to Lea while you still can.' But the man would not be diverted from his course. Whatever happened, he was going to get his messages to Cromford that night. 'Then, if you meet Crooker give him these', said the woman, and took from under her cloak a bunch of St John's wort – a very powerful herb. The traveller put it in his greatcoat pocket along with the primroses and the bluebells and went on his way.

By now the storm was raging so loudly that he could hardly hear himself think. Leaves, twigs and even branches were cascading down onto his head. Trees were thrashing from side to side as though they wanted to pull themselves up by the roots. Stones and boulders were rolling down the bank onto the road, making it hard to keep his footing. On his left he could hear the river raging over rocks and he caught glimpses of the waves and eddies as it threw itself down its course towards Derby.

And then, amongst the mayhem, he heard a new sound from the river – words, a voice: 'Crooker, Crooker, I'm hungry. Give him to me'. From up the bank on his right came a rending sound and a cascade of earth and rocks. A huge, dark shadow loomed towards him and fear filled his heart. In his terror, and without really thinking what he was doing, the traveller reached into his pocket, drew out the bunch of primroses and threw them into the heart of the shadow. With a strange noise – a cross between a shriek and a hiss, the shadow drew back. The man tried to run but he had no strength.

He had only gone a few yards, although it seemed to have taken an age, when he heard the voice again, pleading and begging from the river. 'Crooker, Crooker, I'm hungry. Give him to me', and again something stirred up the bank on his right and the huge dark shadow reached out. Fingers of cold touched him and he reached into his pocket, drew out the bunch of bluebells and threw them into the heart of the shadow. Again the noise, the shriek and hiss, and the shadow drew back.

By now he could see the lights of Cromford just round the bend. Just one more effort and he was safe. But his feet wouldn't move, his strength had gone; it was as if he was in a dream and however fast his legs moved, he did not go anywhere.

'Crooker, Crooker, I'm hungry. Give him to me!' not pleading this time, or begging, but demanding. The river was not going to be denied. Again from the bank on his right came a cascade of earth and rocks and the noise of splintering timber. Something gigantic and black rushed at him and huge arms took him in a cold, strangling grip. He didn't know what he was doing but he must have taken the St John's wort and flung it at Crooker. The noise he heard then made his hair stand on end and his heart stand still. If you imagine someone being torn limb from limb they would make that sort of noise – it contained all the agony and sadness and fear and anguish of every death that has ever happened.

He did not remember picking himself up and running across the bridge, or entering the chapel and slamming the door behind him, but he must have done so for that is where he was found the next morning.

In the daylight, after the storm had abated, the villagers of Cromford came out to see what had happened. They had heard the storm and heard strange noises coming from across the river but, rather than go out to investigate, they had crossed themselves, whispered 'Crooker', and huddled deeper into their beds. Now, as they carefully ventured across the bridge and round the bend, marking the angry waves, the roaring pools and the frustrated murmuring of the river below, they found the wreck of a gigantic ash tree across the road, its branches reaching out like arms and its twigs like fingers grasping the empty air.

That a tree should be blown down by the storm they found easy to understand but how, spaced along the road, they found three bunches of spring flowers – primroses, bluebells and St John's wort – all still as fresh as if they had been picked that morning, was more difficult to explain.

As far as I know, that was the last time Crooker made an appearance. It was over 200 years ago so he may be due to appear again soon. So be careful if you choose to walk along that road at night – for fear of Crooker.

THE ASHBOURNE MINISTER

Many years ago there was a Methodist minister living in Ashbourne. He was a very good preacher and delivered stimulating sermons full of fire and brimstone which kept his congregations on their toes – there was no falling asleep when he was preaching! So he was in great demand to go to preach in neighbouring villages as well. To enable this, he developed the following habit: on Sunday morning he would preach in his own chapel in Ashbourne, then go home and have his dinner, and then, in the afternoon, he'd set off to preach at the evening service at a chapel some-where else in Derbyshire. This worked very well until the events in this story happened.

It was the end of October and the Sunday fell on the 31st, the day superstitious folk call Hallowe'en, when ghosts and spirits are supposed to be about. In those days it wasn't a festival which was marked in Derbyshire though, so the minister did not give the date a second thought.

That morning, as usual, he went and stirred up the good folk of Ashbourne and then went home for his dinner and, quite soon afterwards, he readied himself for the journey to Hartington, where he was booked to preach that evening. He had preached in Hartington many times before and had good friends amongst the chapel folk there so he planned to get there early, in time to have a meal and a friendly discussion with some of them before the service.

But his plans started to go wrong as soon as he set foot in the stable, for his horse was lame. The minister examined its foot and then sent for the farrier who confirmed his fear that the horse could not be ridden that day.

If we were in a similar situation today and it was our car which had broken down, we would probably ring up Hartington and apologise that we couldn't possibly get there because we had no transport, but in those far off times people were not so easily deterred. Rather than let down his congregation, the minister set out to walk. After all, Ashbourne to Hartington is only about ten miles. Today it would be a very pleasant, picturesque hike taking in the length of Dove Dale and on into Mill Dale, Biggin Dale and Wolfescote Dale. Most of the way is on specially prepared paths laid out for walkers with steps cut into the hillsides and boardwalks over some of the wettest places. But, of course, it was all so much more rugged and wild then and, as we have said, it was the end of October, not the best time for a long, wild walk late in the day.

The minister set out under a gloomy sky with clouds so low and thick that he imagined he could reach up and touch them. He reached the hamlet of Thorpe with no problem and took the path under the looming shadow of the hill called Thorpe Cloud. By then the sky had darkened yet more and the air was filled with rain.

As he followed the River Dove the daylight faded entirely, the wind rose, the rain came down heavily, blowing almost horizontally into his face, and the minister could barely see a few feet ahead. He climbed several hills, by now in pitch darkness, stumbled over boulders and slipped in the mud. He began to wonder whether he was on a path or just finding the easiest way between rocks and heather and gorse. He had to admit that he had no idea where he was or in what direction he was heading. The next time he stumbled and slipped, his mind filled with the thought of the cliffs which could be waiting ahead. If he was on the path he would be safe, but he wasn't sure where the path was. In his mind he saw himself walking off the heights of Lover's Leap and remembered the words of a friend who indulged in the new craze of rock-climbing: 'I'm not scared of falling, but I am scared of hitting the ground!' The minister thought about turning round and retracing his steps, but with the rain now coming down in torrents he doubted that he could even do that. He decided that the wisest thing he could do was to find somewhere to shelter – a cave, a shepherd's hut or, best of all, a house. But there wouldn't be any houses anywhere near if he was on his correct path!

As luck would have it he hadn't gone very far when he caught a glimpse of a light off up the hill to the right. It flickered and was lost in the wind and rain. Perhaps he had imagined it. Perhaps it was just a stray ray of light coming through the clouds, but he turned towards it. Then it was there again. As he drew closer it became obvious that it couldn't be a proper house. It was a small, flickery light – a lamp or a candle perhaps. He thought it might be another benighted traveller like himself, cowering under a cliff. But then he stumbled over ruined walls and the hulk of a building took shape around him. Parts of the ancient farmstead were in ruins with hardly one stone on another, parts were in the act of falling down, but one small wing of the building seemed reasonably solid and it was from a window in that part that the light came.

He found the door and banged as loudly as he could. No answer. Perhaps the occupants couldn't hear him above the noise of the gale. He hammered again and, after a pause, he heard the sound of footsteps and then of bolts being drawn back. Peering through the crack in the door was a youngish woman and behind her, holding a lantern in the gloom, a man who was probably her husband. As soon as they saw the minister, half-drowned and battered by the storm and covered in mud where he had slipped and fallen, they almost dragged him into the hallway. They welcomed him and took his wet coat, hat and boots. Then they placed him in front of the fire and gave him a hot drink and simple food to eat.

They were a pleasant young couple and they insisted that the minister could not possibly go further that day for he was several miles from his route and he was unlikely to reach his destination in one piece. He was to stay the night there and hope that the storm had abated by morning so that they could put him safely on his route home, they said.

As they talked, the minister looked round the room in which he now found himself. It was a humble abode with just a few pieces of old furniture, but it had obviously once known better days. He could tell this from the plaster work around the ceiling and the quality of the doors. He could have stood up in the fireplace.

In their conversation his hosts apologised for the dilapidated state of their home and mentioned that they lived there free of charge in return for stopping the rest of it from going to wrack and ruin. When the minister tried to get them to tell him more, they would not and quickly changed the subject. The only explanation they offered him was to say that 'no one wants to live here'. Although the minister tried to get them to explain that statement as well, he could get nothing further from them.

Soon the food and drink and the warmth of the fire began to have its effect and the minister started to yawn, and he was shown upstairs to where a soft bed awaited. It was a huge, old four-poster. As he lay down he wondered what stories that old bed could tell. He thought of the men and women who had laid in it, those who had died and those who had been born. He listened to the storm raging outside and he was asleep in a matter of minutes.

But in the night he woke. Something had disturbed him but he didn't know what. Then he realised he was hungry and thirsty. He remembered that there was some food left from their supper on the kitchen table and thought that the kind pair who had saved him from the storm would not mind if he helped himself. He crept out of the bedroom and down the stairs.

When he was about halfway down he became aware of voices. Not just the two voices of the couple who lived there, but many voices. They seemed to be coming from downstairs in the kitchen. But that was impossible. How could a group of people have come there on a filthy night like this, and why would they? He pushed open the kitchen door and, sure enough, the room was full of finely clad people. Men and women stood in little groups talking and laughing, the table was laden with food and everyone seemed to be enjoying themselves. A tall man, all dressed in green, turned, saw the minister and approached him. 'Come in, friend, and welcome', he said. 'Help yourself to food and drink.' Now, the minister had started to come downstairs in order to get something to eat and drink so this was just what he wanted to hear. He poured himself a mug of drink and piled a plate full of rich food. Somewhere in the back of his mind was an unease, a question about these people and the plentiful food which all seemed so out of place with the room and the couple he had met last night, but these thoughts stayed in those recesses and he carried on helping himself.

But he was a minister, a devout man, and he never ate a meal without saying grace. So when he was ready, he put the plate on the table, placed his hands together, closed his eyes and said:

> Thank you for this drink and food
> Keep me from harm and make me good.
> I hope for Heaven when I die
> And may all devils flee and fly.

And the room fell silent.

When the minister opened his eyes, it was empty – no party goers, no food, no bottles of drink. The kitchen was the tiny room he had seen the previous evening, the table the plain, scrubbed deal without the rich cloths he had seen a moment before. A mouse scuttled behind the wainscot.

He shook himself and a realisation swept over him – he had been dreaming. He had dreamed about being hungry and sleep-walked down the stairs and imagined food and drink in the kitchen. The party had only happened in his sleep. Now he was awake. It was as simple as that. He thought he would tell his hosts about it in the morning,

it would make them laugh. The minister found a drink of water and the chunk of bread he remembered being left over and then went back to bed and fell asleep.

In the morning he awoke to find that the storm had blown itself out, the sky was blue and he was feeling refreshed and ready to make his way back to Ashbourne. Before he left he did tell the young couple about his imaginary adventures in the night but they appeared not to take much heed and he didn't notice the knowing look that passed between them.

And that was the end of the story as far as the minister was concerned. He lived for a good many more years and continued his preaching. He made the journey from Ashbourne to Hartington many more times, but without any more adventures. Sometimes things on the journey would remind him of that trip but he just smiled and went on his way.

Time passed and things changed. If you were to retrace his steps today, you might, eventually, find that old, ruined farmstead, although it is way off the route he was aiming to take. If you did, you probably wouldn't recognise it though. It has changed hands several times since the minister's day and every owner has improved it and fitted it with all the latest conveniences. If it came up for sale today and you wanted to buy it you would have to be a very rich man indeed, for it is a most desirable residence.

And that is all because, ever since the minister said grace before his meal, the reasons that 'no one wants to live here' have all gone away.

Four

TALES OF HEROES

This section features a variety of heroes, including two of the greatest British heroes of all time – King Arthur and Robin Hood. Both are mythical figures who may, or may not, have a basis in history, but it is pretty safe to say that if they did actually live, they didn't do half the things credited to them in folk tales!

The 'real' Arthur is usually identified as a Romano-British warrior of about the sixth century. In the classic tellings, he seems to live perhaps 800 years after that, in the golden age of chivalry and 'knights in armour'. I've compromised. My protagonists might look like knights from the fourteenth century, but just below the surface you can see a Dark-Age warrior.

It is rare for Arthur to venture into the Midlands, but Robin Hood is definitely a Midlands figure. Nottinghamshire proudly bills itself as 'Robin Hood Country' but, as an outlaw, he would have ranged across county boundaries at will.

The other stories in the section deal with people who are definite historical figures – in fact, Florence Nightingale and the people of Eyam have become Derbyshire icons. The events in their stories did happen but the question is, did they happen in the way that the accepted stories tell? I am not going to get into a discussion about that – for the sake of this book it doesn't matter whether Florence Nightingale was the saintly 'Lady with the Lamp', or an old battleaxe who wanted her own way. This is a book of stories, so I am telling the story as it is generally accepted. It is up to other people to delve into the truth.

As the journalist at the end of John Ford's film *The Man Who Shot Liberty Valence* said, 'When the legend becomes fact, print the legend'.

KING ARTHUR AND SIR TERRIBLE

Longdendale is in the far north-west of Derbyshire where it borders onto Cheshire and Lancashire (or now Greater Manchester). It is very much border territory, with all that that implies. It has always been somewhere you go through, not somewhere you go to. In the past, travellers avoided the area if they possibly could but if there was no alternative they hurried through as quickly and quietly as possible, and while they were doing so they kept their weapons handy and any valuables they had hidden away.

In the days before the Industrial Revolution filled the dale with factories, mills and rows of poor houses for the workers, there were just a few villages and the odd wayside inn for travellers on the road through the dale. Off the road there were a few struggling farms and further into the remote moorlands, who knows what there was? Wild animals? Definitely. Dragons? Well, if there were any anywhere it would have been there. Hermits? Bandits? Almost certainly. And sitting on the top of one of the most unreachable hills in the whole area was the castle of Sir Terrible, the feared and fearful ruler of the area.

Sir Terrible was a knight; a huge, powerful, black-hearted knight who thought it was his right to do as he pleased and not give a second thought to what anyone else felt or believed, least of all the humble folk who had the misfortune to live near his stronghold. His castle was as large and powerful as he was, perched on a high cliff with walls stretching out around it like arms, making it impregnable.

Sir Terrible was in the prime of his life but was unmarried. This wasn't because he didn't like women, just the opposite. He just saw no point in limiting himself to one woman when the countryside was full of them! He made use of as many women as he desired. Whenever he felt the need he would descend upon a farm or a village, slay the inhabitants, set fire to the buildings and carry off the most attractive woman in the place. Then, long into the night, her anguished cries would be heard rending the air over the surrounding hills. Anyone within earshot would cover their ears, say a prayer that the woman's sufferings would not last too long, and go on their way as quickly and quietly as they could. The poor woman would never be seen again. This had been going on for many years and there was no one who could do anything about it.

And then King Arthur came to the north-west to fight a battle near Wigan. It was an important battle and he won a decisive victory. The enemy were vanquished and never troubled the country again. After the battle, Arthur stayed on in the area to hold court and people from all over the north-west came to him asking for help and justice and guidance, or perhaps just to pay tribute. Among them came an old woman from Longdendale. Her granddaughter, who was the most beautiful, gentle and best-loved young woman in the valley, had recently been carried off by Sir Terrible. Her parents had been slain and their land laid to waste. The old woman had reason to believe that her granddaughter was still alive, imprisoned in the knight's castle and suffering daily at his hands. The old woman had already told her tale to two noble knights from the locality who had attempted a rescue, only to be slaughtered by Sir Terrible without a second thought.

By now it was late in the day but, after hearing this awful tale, King Arthur wasted no time in buckling on his armour, taking his famous sword Excalibur and, accompanied only by a young squire, riding off towards Longdendale to mete out justice to the renegade knight and rescue the young woman if she was still alive. He took lodgings for the night in a lowly peasant hut where he was told of further dreadful deeds perpetrated by Sir Terrible, so it was very early the next morning that he spurred his horse on towards the evil knight's stronghold.

When the castle came into view, the squire, who had been silent up until now, begged leave to ask a boon of the King:

'Sire, I am young and untried but my father was one of the most noble knights at the court of Uther Pendragon. I may fail and fall at the first hurdle but please grant me this quest. Let me try my hand against Sir Terrible so that I may honour my father and perhaps gain entry into the Fellowship of the Round Table.'

King Arthur had misgivings about granting the squire's wish. If Sir Terrible was as bold a knight as everyone said, he might be sending the young man to his death, but he admired the squire's bravery and his wish to live as a knight, so Arthur sent the squire forth while he stayed back behind some trees.

The young man rode up to the castle gate and hammered loudly on it. The gate opened and out rode Sir Terrible, fully helmeted and armed with his lance ready. The squire exclaimed:

'Villain and treacherous knight, how dare you take innocent and defenceless maidens whom all knights are bound to protect! How dare you keep them here as prisoners in your castle and then kill them when you have done your worst! I am come to make you rue this foul insult to the Order of our good King Arthur. Your cruelties are a stain upon the honour of this fair realm!'

'You young whipper-snapper,' laughed Sir Terrible, 'you'd dare to challenge me? Lead on to yon level patch of green and for your cheek I'll do you the honour of meeting you in fair fight.'

The squire was used to the honour and chivalry of the Knights of the Round Table so, not suspecting foul play, he turned his horse and rode before Sir Terrible towards the patch of level ground where they could engage in fair combat. As soon as the youth's back was turned, Sir Terrible raised his lance, rode at him and caught him full in the back. The squire tumbled from his horse and lay senseless on the ground.

Sir Terrible brought his horse to a halt and made ready to finish off the prone young man. At that moment King Arthur let out a loud shout and stepped out from the trees with his sword in his hand. 'Stay your hand!' he cried. 'That was the most foul stroke that ever I did see, and it will cost you your life.'

Sir Terrible did not recognise the King and did not wait for him to be mounted, but grasped his lance, spurred his horse and rode full at Arthur. King Arthur waited until the last possible moment and then stepped aside. As he did so he brought Excalibur down with all his might. The sword cut through the lance and brought Sir Terrible's horse tumbling to the ground. Then the knight realised who he was facing. He stumbled to his feet. 'You are the King', he said. 'There is only one sword which could have delivered a blow like that; Excalibur. Forgive me Your Majesty. I crave your pardon. I would never have behaved like that if I had known it was you.' But a steely glint came into Arthur's eye. Sir Terrible saw it and turned to flee like the coward he was. Arthur raised Excalibur and brought it down on the evil knight's head. It cut through helmet and armour and the severed head bounced down the hillside, from where Arthur retrieved it. Then the King turned his attention to the squire and saw that he had only been knocked unconscious, so he revived him.

King Arthur and the squire rode to Sir Terrible's castle and banged on the gate. The guard shouted, 'Who dares knock at Sir Terrible's gate? I cannot open it when my master is not here and you would be wise not to be around when he returns!'

'Your master has returned. He is here', shouted Arthur and he tossed the head of Sir Terrible over the gate.

'Who is it that has treated our master so vilely?' asked the guards.

'It is the King', replied Arthur. 'Open the gates and let me in.' The terrified guards threw down their weapons, opened the gates and stood with bowed heads while Arthur and the squire rode into the castle. The King ordered them to free all the captives, which they did. Last of all, out from the dungeons, came the young woman whose rescue had been the reason for the whole quest. Despite her sufferings, she was so beautiful that Arthur immediately complimented her and invited her to become one of the Queen's maidens at court. She curtsied and lowered her eyes and said how honoured she felt, but she was only a simple country maid and she would feel like a bird in a cage if restricted to the court. She would far rather remain in her beloved Longdendale.

King Arthur granted her wish, but he immediately knighted the squire and gave him Sir Terrible's castle as his own and he suggested that the young woman might consent to become the new knight's lady to which everyone, including the maiden, was pleased to agree.

In the following years great changes came over Longdendale. People were no longer frightened to pass near the castle and those in remote hamlets did not lock their doors and dowse their lights when they heard horses in the night. Robbers and outlaws moved away from the area and the new lord and his lady ruled Longdendale justly for many years.

SIR GAWAIN AND THE GREEN KNIGHT

The main event of this story takes place in Staffordshire, but only by a stone's throw. The Green Chapel is at Grabach, which is between the A54 Buxton to Congleton road and the A53 Buxton to Leek road. Before he found the Green Chapel, Gawain must have travelled through Derbyshire and perhaps the castle where he was entertained by 'the Knight's Lady' was in Derbyshire.

County boundaries are artificial and ephemeral things. Although the cores of the old counties have remained constant for centuries, the boundaries move one way and the other like tides, usually for political reasons. Sometimes those boundaries follow real physical features that act as natural barriers – rivers or hilltop ridges – but often they are quite arbitrary. So, people who live in one county sometimes identify more with a town or city in a neighbouring county than with their own county town and go there for their shopping and entertainment. This is particularly true of Derbyshire. People in the north-east of the county naturally turn towards Sheffield and South Yorkshire; in the north-west it is Stockport and Manchester. The south-west around Swadlincote was, until recently, part of the Leicestershire coalfield and the area around Long Eaton and Ilkeston looks to Nottingham – Long Eaton even has Nottingham postcodes. The Peak, though, has always been a place on its own where anything can happen!

It was Christmas time and King Arthur and all the noble Knights of the Round Table were assembled at

Camelot, along with their Ladies. The strength and valour of the knights was well-matched by the beauty and achievements of the ladies. Every day was celebrated with talking and joking; with dancing and singing; with tournaments and jousting. Arthur was a noble king and his knights were the finest that had ever been gathered together in one place, so it was a grand sight.

Now it was New Year's Eve. Arthur and the whole company celebrated the change of year with a service in the chapel and then, in good spirits, they entered the hall ready for a feast. All present exchanged good wishes and gifts and then the first course was served. But Arthur sat quietly and did not eat. He was restless and it had become his custom not to eat until he had been told of a brave deed accomplished by one of his retinue, or of a strange

novelty which took his fancy, or until some strange knight had arrived and challenged one of the Round Table to a tournament.

The second course was heralded in with drums and trumpets, banners and flags, and with it came a most amazing sight. Into the hall rode a knight – a knight such as they had never seen before. He was a man, but a man of huge size; taller than any of the knights there present. And not only was he tall, he was large with it. His chest, his thighs, his arms were all massive. His hair was thick and bushy and cut off straight at his shoulders and his beard reached to his chest. He was wearing no armour, just a long, straight robe and he carried no weapons other than a large, knobbly, holly branch and a huge axe. The horse he was riding was equally impressive – it had to be to carry this giant of a man! But this was not the most amazing thing about him. The knights and ladies could not take their eyes off him because he was green all over – his skin, his hair, his clothing and his horse; all a bright, lizard-skin green.

The Green Knight rode through the hall and halted before the dais. 'Who is the leader of this throng?' he asked, 'For I wish to have conversation with him.' He looked into the eyes of all the knights present and they all returned his gaze silently, too amazed and awed to speak. Was this a human man or a phantasm? Or had he come from the land of Fairie?

At last Arthur spoke up, 'I am the King here,' he said, 'and you are welcome to join us in our feast if you come in peace. If you are looking for trouble and fighting then you are also welcome, for you will find the best knights in the land assembled here before you.'

The Green Knight replied:

'Fear not, I do, indeed, come in peace and this holly branch is a symbol of that. If I had come looking for trouble I have a plentiful supply of armour and weapons in my castle and I would have happily challenged any one of your warriors for they look like nothing but beardless youths. No, wherever I have travelled I have heard talk of the bravery and honour and wisdom of the people of this place and I have come to see if what I have heard is correct.'

A murmur from around the room assured him that it was. The knight continued:

'Then I have a Christmas jest to try on you. Is there anyone here who will agree to play with me in this game? Here is my axe, I will freely grant it to anyone who will swap me stroke for stroke with it. And I will bear the first stroke. Let him strike me as hard as he like as I stand here unarmed. The only condition is that he comes to me a year and a day from now to be repaid by my stroke.'

The court listened in amazement, for how could the Green Knight possibly repay a stroke with such an axe, for surely the first one would be deadly. No one moved and they squirmed in their seats as the Green Knight looked into their hearts. At length, Arthur could bear the humiliation no more and rose to his feet.

'Give me the axe and I will smite you such a blow that you never rise again', he said. The Green Knight calmly handed Arthur the axe and bared his neck. Arthur hefted the blade in his hands.

Then Gawain rose to his feet. 'Sire,' he said, 'it is not fitting that you should take part in such a trivial game. It is far beneath your position. I pray you to allow me to take your place. What if this is some trick of magic and betrayal? The court dare not lose you, but I would be no loss. Let me take your place.' The rest of Arthur's court murmured their agreement so Arthur handed the axe to Gawain and returned to his seat.

The Green Knight turned to Gawain and asked him his name and lineage. Gawain proudly told him and then asked the knight in turn his name and title and the place where he lived, but the knight refrained from telling him. 'First you must strike the stroke and then I will tell you where to find me. It is better that you do not know too much too soon', he said. Then he knelt on the floor, bared his neck again and readied himself for Gawain's stroke. Gawain lifted the axe and dropped it lightly onto the Green Knight's neck. It was a small stroke but it cut through skin and flesh and bone and in a shower of blood the head leapt from the neck and rolled across the floor. The Green Knight made no sign of distress, he did not fall and he made no sound. He simply reached forward and picked up the head by the hair. With blood dripping from the head and spurting from his own neck, he mounted his horse, turned, and saluted the multitude. The face looked at Gawain. The Knight then said:

Be sure to keep the other half of the bargain. Next New Year's Day, be sure to meet me and to allow me to give you such a blow as you have given me. You will have no trouble in finding me, for I am the Knight of the Green Chapel. Just ask and you will find me. If you do not meet me at the appointed time you will be branded a traitor and a coward.

With that, the knight turned and rode from the hall, leaving the knights astonished and the ladies in a faint.

King Arthur did not let his wonder and amazement show but spoke to the Queen. 'That was a fitting trick for Christmas when we delight in mirth and merriment and ballads of brave deeds', he said. 'And now a wonder has occurred, I will dine.' He took his seat next to Gawain and commanded him to hang the axe on the wall behind the dais. The court spent the next few days in their celebrations until Twelfth Night signalled the return to normal life. But Gawain was weighed down by the knowledge of what was to face him in a year's time.

Time passed and the New Year grew older. Lent gave way to Easter; spring became summer and, in turn, blossomed into to autumn and Michaelmas. Gawain stayed at Camelot until All Hallows, when the court held a feast in his honour. Arthur reminded Gawain of his quest and all the knights assembled to wish him luck. The ladies also assembled to wish him 'God Speed', for every woman in the court loved the noble, chivalrous Gawain and they kissed him and shed tears. The next morning Gawain dressed himself in his finest armour, strapped on his weapons, including the axe he had taken from the

Green Knight, mounted his horse and set out to find the Green Chapel.

He rode through the land of Logres and north to Holyhead, where he turned inland towards Chester. He crossed the forests of the Wirral and then followed the Monk's Road east and then south into the land of the Peakrills – a wild, uninhabited place which was unknown to him or any of Arthur's knights. He battled giants and dragons, fought wolves and wild beasts – bears, bulls and boars. Wherever he went, he asked for news of the Green Chapel. No one knew its exact location but they always sent him on into lands which became more and more remote and desolate.

On Christmas Eve, Gawain found himself in a large, thick forest. He prayed to the Mother of God for a sign and soon found himself confronted by the moat and walls of a rich castle. Gawain rode round it until he found the drawbridge and gateway. He wondered which noble knight could live there unknown to any in Arthur's court. He rode onto the drawbridge and hailed. A porter looked over the battlements and after an exchange of words, the gates swung open. Gawain entered and was met by squires and pages, who helped him from his horse which was stabled and fed. They led Gawain into a fine hall where he was welcomed by the castle's owner, a large, robust, red-faced knight who looked like a natural leader of men. The knight had Gawain shown to a fine bedroom where he was helped from his armour and dressed in rich robes so that he looked almost like a god. Gawain was then feasted and cosseted and when the knight learned that he was

Gawain of the Court of King Arthur, he was invited to spend the Christmas holiday with his host.

Then Gawain was introduced to the knight's lady, who was the fairest woman he had ever seen – fairer even than the Lady Guinevere, Gawain thought. He greeted her with a knightly kiss and she blushed fetchingly. The lady was accompanied by an elderly woman who said little but looked at Gawain strangely. Over the Christmas holiday, Gawain danced many dances with the knight's lady and they sang songs together and asked each other riddles, but he never treated her less than chivalrously.

When the holiday was ended, the knight took Gawain aside and said he was honoured to have had him as a guest, but why had he left Arthur's court at such a time? Gawain then told him about his errand and the dreadful debt he had to repay at the Green Chapel. Could the knight help him find the place, he asked, for he had to be there on the first day of the New Year. Then the knight let out a huge laugh.

'You have nothing to worry about', he said. 'You can remain here with us and rest comfortably in your bed. On New Year's Day itself I can direct you to the place you seek and you will be there by mid-morning, for it is not far away.'

The knight then told Gawain that he should rest and prepare himself for the trial which awaited him. He, himself, would go hunting the next morning but Gawain should sleep in and take his food in bed. The knight's lady herself would sit with him and wait on him. 'Let us make a pledge,' said the knight, 'that whatever I kill in the forest I will give to you and you, in turn, will grant me whatever you win while I'm away.' The agreement was made and the two knights drank to it.

Early the next morning the knight and his retinue left for the hunt. Gawain slept on. He was barely awake when he heard his door opening. Through a half-closed eye he saw the knight's lady enter the room. Her hair was uncovered and she was only lightly dressed. Gawain feigned sleep and the lady sat by his bedside and watched. At length, Gawain pretended to wake and to be surprised to find the lady sitting by his bed. Throughout the day she stayed with Gawain and waited on him and they talked and laughed. It was an innocent flirtation, but Gawain found it hard not to acknowledge his feelings. Towards evening the lady left so that Gawain could prepare himself for the knight's return. As she said her farewells, she bent and looked Gawain in the eye and kissed him full on the lips, and it was not just a polite kiss…

At evening time the knight and his retinue returned with great fanfare and a feast was served. When all had eaten and drunk, the knight ordered his kill for the day to be presented to Gawain as their agreement had been. Onto the floor before Gawain was thrown a fine deer. 'And what have you won, Gawain, to give to me in return?' asked the knight. Gawain rose, embraced the knight and planted a kiss on his lips. 'Nothing but a sisterly kiss', he said, and the whole room burst into laughter.

The next morning, the knight again rose early, prayed, breakfasted, and went hunting. That day the hunting was good. They chanced to rouse a huge, old boar that put up a good fight and gored several dogs before the knight eventually despatched it. Gawain again lay in bed and was again visited by the knight's lady, who was dressed in a fetching robe which showed off her figure to its best. She talked to him softly and soothingly.

'What did you learn yesterday?' she asked. Gawain said that he did not think he had learned anything. 'Did you not learn of love and kissing?' she asked. 'Would you not like to practise more?' Gawain denied any such inclination and they spent the rest of the morning in polite conversation but when the lady left, she insisted on another kiss which Gawain could not help but grant.

That night the lord presented Gawain with the carcass of the huge boar and in return Gawain embraced him and planted a second kiss on his lips.

On the third day, the hunting was even better. The retinue enjoyed the thrill of the chase and made several kills. At the close of the day they made their way home, tired but thrilled. Gawain, meanwhile, awoke to find the lady wearing her most costly robes with a coronet on her head. She was the finest sight a man could wake to! She addressed him on the subject of love and asked about his previous lovers. When he denied having had any, she did not believe him. Talk of love can easily lead to deeds of love and Gawain hid his feelings under the blankets. As the day wore on, the lady tried with all her womanly ways to seduce Gawain and when she failed she said he must be betrothed. Gawain found it very difficult to resist the lady's charms. He said he would willingly make love to her, for she was the most beautiful woman he had seen in his life, but he could not because of the debt he owed her husband and because of the deed he had to do the next day.

'Then I will leave you here and return to my room with a broken heart', she said. 'But will you not give me one small token so that I may have something to remember you by? A glove perhaps?'

Gawain again refused but the lady said, 'Then if you will not give me a gift as a remembrance, I will give you one', and she held out a ring of gold with a large red stone mounted in it. Gawain refused it. It was too much. 'Then take this lace from my girdle', she said. 'It is of no value, but it will remind you of me.' She drew from under her gown a lace of golden-green silk and told him that she had woven it with her own hand. But again Gawain refused. Then she told him that this small, insignificant lace had the power to make its wearer invincible. No man could harm him who wore it. Gawain thought about the return blow in the Green Chapel and took the lace. Then the lady kissed him for the third time and departed.

That evening the knight returned as usual and the ex-change of venison and boar carcasses for the kiss was duly carried out. But Gawain said nothing about the lace. The next morning, being New Year's Day, Gawain dressed him-self in his armour and fastened the silken lace around his waist. He bade a sad farewell to all and gave a formal salute to the castle and, accompanied by a guide, rode off to his fate. They rode through rugged, uninhabited countryside until, after an hour or so, the guide stopped.

'You are very near the place,' he said, 'but I beg you to think twice before you continue. Here dwells a knight who challenges all who pass by and in many years he has never been defeated. No one will think less of you if you turn and leave quietly.' But Gawain insisted that he would think less of himself. He took his farewell of his guide and went on. He could see no sign of a castle or a green chapel. Then he came into a large green space in which was a mound. Gawain could sense that this was a magical place and knew it must be the fabled Green Chapel. As he sat on his horse, he heard the sound of metal on stone and knew that somewhere close at hand weapons were being sharpened. And then, out of a cleft in the rock rode the Green Knight.

They greeted each other and the knight complimented Gawain on being brave enough to keep his half of the bargain. Without more ado, they agreed that the deed should be done. Gawain dismounted from his horse, removed his helmet, and knelt with bared neck. The Green Knight raised his axe and brought it towards Gawain's neck with all his might. But before it could nick one hair on the back of Gawain's head, he halted it in mid-air. Gawain, however, flinched.

The Green Knight scolded him, 'You are Gawain!' he said sternly. 'You do not fear any man in this land and yet you flinch from my blade before it has even touched you! Shame on you. Did I flinch when you struck your stroke?'

Gawain apologised and explained that it was just a reflex reaction and if the Green Knight swung again, not a nerve would twitch. A second time the Knight struck and again he halted the stroke just before it landed, and Gawain stood as steady as an oak tree.

'Enough!' he cried. 'Stop playing with me. We had an agreement that we would each strike one stroke. No more empty swings. Strike me and be done with it!'

For the third time the Green Knight lifted the axe and this time he let it fall under its own weight. It nicked Gawain's skin and blood flowed. As soon as Gawain saw this, he put on his helmet and drew his sword. 'The bargain is done', he said. 'If you strike again you have broken your word and I am free to defend myself.'

The Green Knight stepped back and lowered his axe:

Fear not the bargain is complete. We will exchange no more blows. I would have landed no blows at all once I saw that you were man enough to keep your half of the bargain. That first feint was for my wife, whom you kissed and gave me the kiss. The second which did not land, likewise. The third blow which did land was for the golden green silk lace which you wear and did not disclose to me. Well I know your courting of my wife, for it was I who sent her to try you. You must be the most honest, chivalrous knight there is, for none other could withstand her charms. You failed not in withstanding her love making or in your honesty in giving me the kisses you won, but you did fail in loving your own life so much that you kept the charm without telling me. But for that I forgive you. Keep it now and wear it with pride. Now it would please me if you would return to my castle and make your peace with my wife, who is feeling slighted by your rebuttal of her charms, and also to meet with your aunt. For that is who the old lady is – your aunt Morgan le Fay. She who was once the mistress of Merlin and is Arthur's half-sister. It was she who sent me to Camelot to try this jest. Her aim was to frighten Guinevere and to bring shame on the court of Arthur. But, because of your honesty, her plan has failed.

Gawain refused the offer and asked for his regards to be forwarded to the two good ladies. Then he asked the Green Knight what his true name was. 'I am called Bernlak de Hautdesert', he replied.

'Then, Bernlak de Hautdesert, may I take my leave of you and return from whence I came?' And Gawain turned his horse towards the south and made his long journey home to Camelot where there was great rejoicing at his safe return and where he had to tell the tale of his adventures over and over again.

ROBIN HOOD AND LITTLE JOHN

When bold Robin Hood was about eighteen years old,
He chanced for to meet Little John,
A jolly brisk blade, just fit for his trade,
For he was a sturdy young man.

Traditional ballad

Robin Hood, possibly the most famous hero of English folklore is, of course, mostly associated with Nottinghamshire. For a man of his time he was well travelled though: in some stories he went to the King's Court in London; he is supposed to have caught a ship from Robin Hood's Bay in North Yorkshire; and he died at Kirklees Abbey in West Yorkshire. There are a host of places in Derbyshire which carry his name, ranging from tiny wells and caves to the huge rocky outcrop near Bakewell known as Robin Hood's Stride.

Perhaps we can assume that if his enemy the Sheriff of Nottingham got too close, Robin would leave his head-quarters at the Major Oak in Sherwood Forest and venture far outside that area to Barnsdale Forest, near Doncaster, or into the bleak wilderness of the Peak. It is almost certain that at least some of his 'merry men' must have been:

> Derbyshire born and Derbyshire bred,
> Strong in the arm and wick in the head.

One such was his right-hand man, Little John. This is the well-known story of their first meeting.

Robin Hood was about eighteen years old and had not been an outlaw for long. He was still putting his band to-gether. He'd found some good, dependable men and sent some bad, untrustworthy men on their way, but what he re-ally wanted was a lieutenant, a right-hand man who could take charge when he wasn't there, or who could command one group of men while he commanded another.

One morning Robin was walking through the fringes of Sherwood Forest when he came to a stream. It wasn't very wide or very deep, but Robin didn't want to get wet. Over the stream was a bridge made from the trunk of a fallen tree. Just as Robin approached one end of the bridge, an-other man approached the other end. Robin took a step onto his end of the bridge and the other man took a step onto his. They stopped and looked at each other. There was no way they could both cross at once as the tree trunk was too narrow to allow them to pass. One of them had to give way.

'Give way, stranger!' shouted Robin.

'No, you give way yourself!' replied the other man in a broad Derbyshire accent.

'Stand back or I'll show you how Nottingham men fight!' said Robin.

'Then you're a coward!' replied the other. 'You threaten me with your longbow and arrows and I've only got this staff to protect myself. Go on then, shoot me and welcome.' The man stood on his end of the bridge and spread his arms wide, offering Robin his chest as a target he could hardly miss, for this man was huge. He must have been nearly 7ft tall and broad with it.

'I won't be called a coward or a cheat by you or by anyone else!' shouted Robin 'You stay there while I cut a staff and we will have a fair fight.'

Robin ran into the thicket and cut himself a stout staff and then, putting his bow aside, the two men advanced into the centre of the bridge. After a few trial strokes, Robin managed to crack the stranger on the head but it had little effect other than to make him fight even harder. The next stroke knocked Robin right off the bridge and into the stream.

'Where are you now, my little cock sparrow?' laughed the stranger.

'Why, I'm here in the flood', spluttered Robin dragging himself from the stream. Once back on dry land, Robin Hood took a horn from his belt and blew a loud blast. After a few minutes the wood came alive with rustlings and shouts and from every quarter, armed men appeared and gathered round Robin and the stranger.

'What's the matter, master?' they asked. 'What's been happening?' When Robin explained that the stranger had toppled him into the stream, they drew their swords and were ready to avenge their leader, but Robin stopped them. 'Don't harm him,' he said, 'for he is a doughty fighter and would be a good recruit to our band.'

Robin then asked the man his name and was told that he was John Little, a nailer from Hathersage. This name, coming from so huge a man, raised a peal of laughter. He said that he would be proud to join the band so they all made their way back to the outlaw's camp where a pair of deer were roasted. Then a fresh keg of ale was opened and

a feast prepared. That night, John Little was re-christened Little John and he became Robin's most trusted friend and companion through many, many adventures.

Little John was also there at Robin Hood's death. Robin was betrayed by his cousin, the Prioress of Kirklees Hall, who, under the guise of bleeding him to restore him to health, bled him until he was nearly dead. Robin then called for his bow and shot an arrow to mark his final resting place.

With Robin dead, the outlaw band fell apart. The merry men gradually drifted away and Little John decided to return to Hathersage to end his days with his family. This he did and when he died, in the cottage where he had been born, he was buried in Hathersage churchyard.

I know that is true because if you go to the churchyard today, you can still see a gravestone marking the spot. It stands within railings and the inscription reads:

Here lies buried Little John, the friend and lieutenant of Robin Hood. He died in a cottage (now destroyed) to the east of the churchyard. The grave is marked by this old headstone and footstone and is underneath this old yew tree.

And that grave is a good 13ft long!

ROBIN HOOD'S PICKING RODS

This story takes place in Longdendale, in the far north-west of Derbyshire. It is still one of the most remote parts of the Peak and the road from Hadfield over the

Woodhead Pass (now the A628) to Sheffield is one of the highest in the Pennines and is often closed by bad weather. Think how remote it must have been in Robin Hood's day! For that reason, it was one of the places he and his men would retreat to if the Sheriff of Nottingham made things too uncomfortable in Sherwood Forest. As well as being relatively safe, it was also good for hunting. It was said the forest was so thick that squirrels could leap from branch to branch all the way from Mottram to Woodhead, never touching the ground. And there was also the chance of booty. The Abbots of Basingwerk often travelled between nearby Glossop and their abbey on the North Wales coast near Holywell, carrying their money and valuables with them and they were good prey – a good source of income which could be redistributed to the poor.

When the events in this story happened, Robin and some of his men, including Little John, Friar Tuck, Will Scarlet, Much the miller's son and several others, had been staying in Longdendale for several weeks and were becoming bored. The hunting was too easy and they were looking for adventure in the way that young men with nothing to do will. One morning, as they were roaming through the forest, they became aware of a loud sobbing and crying coming from somewhere nearby. They went to investigate and came upon a handsome young man who was laying on the ground bemoaning his cruel fate. When Robin and his men appeared, the young gentleman clambered to his feet and drew his sword, although he would have stood no chance against such a force. Robin calmed him and asked what was wrong, why was the young man so troubled?

He replied that he was betrothed to a beautiful maiden who loved him dearly but her guardian – her grim old uncle, the baron – had forbidden their union, and shut her up in his castle. This was just the excuse for action Robin and his men were looking for. They were outraged that the baron should interfere with true love. Some of the men were for storming the castle immediately, while others thought they should lay siege to it. They had as many ideas as they had heads, but Robin had the coolest. He said that an outright attack might imperil the maiden – they had no idea what the uncle might do or what forces he had at his command – so he suggested a plan of his own. Friar Tuck was sent as an emissary to persuade the baron to set the girl free.

The baron would not negotiate with a band of robbers though. 'Get you away from here you fat-bellied, shaven-headed churchman', he shouted. 'What do you know about lovers? What do you know about the feelings of young maidens? Your vows should ensure that you leave young maidens well alone!'

This did not go down well with Friar Tuck for, shaven-headed churchman though he was, he had been known to kiss many a pretty maiden and he had an eye for a beautiful face and a well-filled gown.

'Fat-bellied churchman, indeed!' grumbled the friar. 'And who are you to talk about maidens and lovers? It must have been an age since any woman looked at such an ugly reptile as you!'

The baron was not used to being spoken to in such a way and he was furious. He ordered his retainers to seize the friar and throw him into the dungeon. But before they could lay hands on him, Friar Tuck raised his staff and lay about the baron's servants, cracking heads left, right and centre. The baron was so angry that he grew red in the face and spluttered and choked so much that Friar Tuck burst out laughing and said, 'Calmly now baron, or your anger will carry you to an early grave. Call off your men and let me leave or, I vow, I will lay my staff around your own ears!'

Seeing that he was beaten, the baron paused to think and came up with an alternative method of getting his own way. First he agreed that he had been bettered in the fight and he consented to set the maiden free and allow her marriage to her handsome lover, but there were conditions... The foresters, of whose shooting prowess he had heard so much, had to prove their worth by shooting their arrows at some well known standing stones from a hillock he would point out to them. Friar Tuck knew nothing of the places the baron was talking of but knew that all the outlaws were excellent shots so he agreed, not realising the distances involved. The baron chuckled to himself at the impossible task he had set and which had been accepted. He would get his own way after all, as he usually did.

The time for the shooting display arrived and the baron led the company to the appointed place, attended by many nobles from round about and crowds of local people. The handsome youth on whose behalf Robin had intervened was quite dismayed, for he knew the sites the baron meant and thought the feat was impossible – surely no one could shoot accurately over so great a distance? But little did he know the skill of Robin Hood and his men.

Robin stepped up to the mark first, fitted an arrow into his bow, and let fly. The arrow flew straight and true and hit the stone with such force that it left a groove which can still be seen to this day. Robin was followed by Little John and then the rest of his men and none failed to hit the stone. When they had all shot, Robin asked for the young woman to be brought forth to join her lover but still the baron tried to renege on the bargain. He sought to make another deal with Robin Hood. 'If,' he said, 'you can throw down the great stone that stands on Werneth Low then, not only will I allow the young couple to marry, but I will give them houses and lands and a dowry into the bargain. But if you fail then the marriage is off and you will join the young man in my dungeon.'

Robin accepted the challenge without a second thought and the whole company climbed to the summit of Werneth Low where the gigantic boulder stood. This rock was almost the height of a man and it looked as though it had stood there since the world began. In the past many men had tried to move it, singly or in groups, but none had managed to even make it rock. The baron knew his bargain was safe. Robin Hood took a quick look at the stone, removed his jerkin, flexed his muscles and lifted the huge boulder clear of the ground and then above his head! Then he hurled it into the distance.

After that, with the deed being witnessed by so many people, the baron could not possibly go back on his word. The young couple were duly married and lived a long and happy life on the lands which the baron gave them.

Robin and his men stayed on for the wedding and then returned to their old haunts in Sherwood Forest to continue their ongoing battle with the Sheriff of Nottingham.

The places in this story are still there; you can visit them. The stones at which the merry men shot their arrows are now called Robin Hood's Picking Rods in memory of the feat. They are along a track about two miles south of Charlesworth. No one knows quite what they are or what they were for. The hillock, or tumulus, they shot from is called the Butts. The boulder that Robin threw from the top of Werneth Low landed in the River Tame near the Woods of Arden at Bredbury, which is a good three or four miles away as the arrow flies. It is still there and people know it as Robin Hood's Stone.

EYAM, THE PLAGUE VILLAGE

The story of the brave inhabitants of the little village of Eyam (pronounced 'Eem') is another tale which I could not omit from this collection. It is, arguably, the best known Derbyshire story of all. It is a difficult story to tell though, because we don't know how much of it is fact and how much has been invented or improved to make a good tale. It is so well known and so widely accepted that I could almost be subject to prosecution for slander if I dared to suggest that it is not all absolute, gospel truth and, maybe, all the villagers were not so saintly!

And so I will tell the story as it is generally told, for, after all, this is a book of stories.

It was at the end of August 1665 that George Vicars, the village tailor in Eyam, took delivery of yet another parcel of cloth and old clothes from his supplier in London. He had been doing this for years but recently old clothes were in far greater supply because a dreadful plague was raging in the city and people were dying in their hundreds. If they were dead, they had no more need of clothes and relatives sold them to raise much-needed money.

A few of the more educated people of Eyam had heard a little bit about this but it seemed to be of no relevance to them. Nothing that happened that far away could possibly have any affect on them, could it? Even when the king died, it was months before they noticed any difference!

The weather had been very wet and the packages had not been well wrapped so the cloth was damp when it arrived in Eyam. Vicars took it and hung it in front of his fire to dry before he started to work on it. In fact, he never got further than drying the cloth for, within days, he was taken ill with a raging fever, he was delirious and vomiting, and there were strange lumps in his armpits and groin. Within the week he was dead.

By the end of September, five more people had died with the same symptoms, including the vicar's two stepsons and his employer. In October a further twenty-three villagers died in the same way. By now they knew that they were in the grip of the plague – the Black Death that had ravaged cities all across Europe. How and why had it come to their remote corner of Derbyshire? In those days, no one knew anything of germs or viruses or contagion. They couldn't possibly guess that the fact that George Vicars had started itching as soon as the cloth started drying, because fleas carrying the plague virus had jumped out of the cloth and bitten him, was anything to do with the illness. It must be either the work of God or of the Devil!

The populace dosed themselves with concoctions of herbs to relieve the symptoms. They washed their houses with vinegar and when someone became ill, they let their blood. It came out black and vile-smelling, with a greenish scum on it.

Then winter set in and the death toll shrank, but with spring and the warmer weather the 'wrath' returned. Villagers were terrified. Some were for fleeing to safe places – to Sheffield perhaps. It is likely that a few of the local gentry who had other houses to go to and the cash to pay for moving did leave, but for the ordinary humble folk of the area there was nowhere to go and no way of leaving.

By now they knew what it was that was affecting them and they knew that if they did leave their homes and mingle with the outside world, they were in danger of spreading the disease. This is when they made their heroic decision. They would quarantine themselves in the village. No one would be allowed to leave and no one would be allowed to enter. (In fact, once word got out it is unlikely that anyone would have dared to enter! In less civilised parts of Europe it is possible that bands from outside might have razed the village to the ground and slaughtered the inhabitants as a 'final solution'.)

The plan to quarantine the village was instigated by the rector, the Revd William Mompesson, with the support of his predecessor, the Revd Thomas Stanley. Mompesson urged his congregation to draw strength from their faith. He quoted the gospel of St John: 'Greater love hath no man than this, that a man lay down his life for his friends'.

He put forward a three-part plan. The first thing was that when someone died they should be buried immediately and as close to home as possible – in their gardens probably. This meant that they did not have to wait for the sexton to dig graves in consecrated ground and the bodies did not have to be transported through the village.

The second suggestion was that people should not congregate indoors together. For that reason, he moved the church services out of the church and into Cucklett Delf, a local beauty spot much used by courting couples.

Lastly, and perhaps of most importance, they set up a *cordone sanitaire* around the village, a line which would not be crossed. The people from neighbouring communities also played their part in making the quarantine work – perhaps out of kindness, perhaps out of self-interest. So that the Eyam villagers had no excuse for leaving their homes, they brought food and other supplies to the edge of the area to be collected. The people of Eyam, not wanting charity, insisted on paying for this and left the coins in jars of vinegar to keep off the infection.

Legend has it that only one old woman from Eyam broke the cordon – she ventured into Tideswell market but was recognised and chased out of the village in a hail of stones. One young man ventured to come the other way. Rowland Torre was in the habit of meeting a young Eyam woman called Emmott Sydall in Cucklett Delf. They were in love and something as simple as death and disease was not going to prevent them seeing each other. They continued to meet in the Delf but they kept their distance and called to each other across the rocks until, one day, Emmott ceased to appear. She had fallen victim to the disease.

In Eyam, as in London, the plague continued into 1666. In London that year, there was a great fire and we are taught that that was the main reason the plague ceased – the houses which harboured the rats which had been host to the infected fleas were destroyed, so breaking the cycle. There was no great fire in Eyam, but by the autumn of that year the plague was considered ended there too, and people returned to as normal a life as possible. Figures vary, but up to two-thirds of the population may have died. One of the last was Mompesson's wife.

How does a community put itself back together after an ordeal like that? I cannot imagine. But Eyam did, and there are still some of the same families living there. If you look into the front gardens of the houses along the main street you can see plaques commemorating the plague victims who lived and died in each individual house and a church service is held every year in Cucklett Delf on the last Sunday in August, which is known a Plague Sunday.

So Eyam has come to terms with its history by marketing it, by telling the story. It may be a story we would do well to remember in the not too distant future, if and when a natural or man-made disaster again threatens the population. It can happen in reality, not just in science fiction!

THE LADY WITH THE LAMP
THE STORY OF FLORENCE NIGHTINGALE

Florence Nightingale: an anagram of 'flit on cheering angel'

Florence Nightingale is commemorated in Derby by a statue outside the Derby Royal Infirmary, a nurse's home and a pub. She is also claimed for Derbyshire although she did not really ever live full-time in the county. She was born in Florence, hence her name, and on their return to England her parents bought a house in Hampshire. However, Florence and her sister spent every summer at Lea Hurst, near Matlock, a house their father had inherited from a relation of his wife. Florence's father had been born William Shore, but he changed his surname to Nightingale to honour that relative, 'Mad Peter' Nightingale.

'Mad Peter' had inherited Lea Hurst from his father, also Peter, who had made his fortune through lead mining. 'Mad Peter' was given his nickname because of his lifestyle of gambling, heavy drinking and horse riding, but he was also a very successful businessman. He was into lead smelting and hat making. He also had an arm of Richard Arkwright's Cromford Canal extended up to his own cotton spinning mill, but when Arkwright successfully sued him for breach of his patent, he switched to spinning wool.

I have based my retelling of Florence Nightingale's story on the version told in a pre-First World War encyclopaedia for children. Modern thinking tends to portray her as a more 'difficult' character.

Florence Nightingale was a pretty little girl who lived in a beautiful park in the English countryside. Like most little girls she loved to play with her dolls, but instead of just dressing and undressing them, and combing their hair, and giving them dolls' tea parties, Florence loved to pretend that she was a nurse and that her dolls were ill, or had been dreadfully injured in some terrible accident. She would give them medicines or make bandages and dress their wounds. As she grew older, she began to do the same with her pets, particularly the family dog, and then, when she was older still, she started to visit the poor people who lived on her father's estate and tried to help them in the same way.

Little Florence grew into a fine young lady and, as was the custom with people of her class in those days, there came the day when she was presented at court. This marked the change between being a child and becoming an adult. It was a time for parties and balls and being introduced to other well-to-do families and to eligible young men. Most girls loved all this and tried to catch a fine young man to marry, but not Florence. She did not enjoy it at all and, rather than go to parties, she would sneak off to visit one of the London hospitals.

Nursing, in those days, was not something young ladies went in for. Hospitals and medicine were not for the well-to-do. In fact, nurses were thought of as only slightly above prostitutes, and hospitals were more likely to kill you than heal you! Very little was known about hygiene or germs or of how diseases were spread. Doctors treated their patients and carried out operations wearing their everyday clothes and without washing their hands. And there were no anaesthetics!

Hearing that medicine was more advanced on the Continent, Florence went to Germany and then to Paris to visit hospitals there. She learned a lot and, on her return to England, tried to put what she had learned into practice, against the wishes of the established, male medical profession. It was almost impossible for her to achieve anything.

Then war broke out in the far away Crimea. Britain was fighting against Russia. Many people in England only heard of the glory. Even disasters like the Charge of the Light Brigade were presented as glorious, even though they resulted in British soldiers being slaughtered needlessly. The whole war was a victory of 'spin' over reality. Florence Nightingale saw that this was her opportunity to put her ideas into action.

Against the wishes of the military powers-that-be, Florence and forty nurses went to the British base of Scutari and took over the military hospital there. Far from being a place where people were healed, it was a place where wounded soldiers were sent to die. If their wounds didn't kill them, infections picked up in the hospital did. Under Nightingale's command, the place was cleaned and comfortable beds were provided. The nurses tended the soldiers and dressed their wounds frequently. Florence Nightingale

herself ceaselessly patrolled the hospital wards talking to
the patients and making sure everything was done that
could be. Because of her night time patrols, she became
known as 'the Lady with the Lamp'.

It is said that when she arrived in the Crimea, 42 per
cent of the wounded died. When she had been there for a
short while, this dropped to 2 per cent. In all she treated
about 10,000 soldiers.

Her fame spread in England and she became a hero. When the time came for her to return to England, the Navy sent a man-of-war to carry her home and a collection raised £50,000, intended to be a present for her own use. But Florence did not want the limelight and she returned home to her father's house quietly and unannounced. With the money she founded a home to train nurses in her methods.

The encyclopaedia sums up her story by saying:

The little girl who had nursed the sheep dog and bandaged her dolls now stood forth as England's Angel of Pity and as long as England's history is written the name of Florence Nightingale will shine in golden letters on the page.

THE RUNAWAY TRAIN
THE STORY OF JOHN AXON

The story of John Axon deserves to be remembered as the English equivalent of the great American railway tales:

The runaway train came down the track, her whistle wide
    and her throttle back,
And she blew, blew, blew, blew, blew.

Hit record by Michael Holiday, 1956.

This is another true story and the most recent event included here. As such, there may be people who read this and leap up and shout, 'No, it wasn't like that!' or 'No, our

John didn't do that!' But I will repeat something I've said several times already – I am telling a story.

The story of John Axon did not happen long ago but it has already become folklore, largely due to the BBC Radio ballad put together by Ewan McColl, Peggy Seeger and Charles Parker in 1958, just a short while after the event happened.

American folklore (and popular music) is full of songs and stories about railways and railwaymen: 'the Midnight Special', 'the Wabash Canonball', 'Chattenooga Choo Choo', 'Casey Jones', and of course, the one we all remember from *Children's Favourites*, 'the Runaway Train'. The English tradition is sadly lacking in such; I have come across just a couple of songs written to celebrate or commemorate the opening of a particular railway line, but they were ephemeral items which never caught on.

John Axon, called Jack by his mates, was an engine driver; a heroic job in the 1950s, the thing every schoolboy aspired to do. Jack had been a railwayman for forty years, working his way up through all the different jobs and grades one needed until he reached the pinnacle – the actual driver of the engine. He worked for the GCR, the Great Central Railway, and was based at the Edgeley Engine Shed at Stockport. Jack's route took him out into Derbyshire, driving his trains through some of the most spectacular countryside in England. It was not straightforward engine driving; not racing along long, straight lines, but making his way over viaducts, through cuttings and tunnels, round sharp bends and up and down steep inclines. The driver had to be on his toes. Jack loved it.

At four o'clock in the morning on 9 February 1957, Jack climbed out of his bed, dressed, picked up his snap and made his way to work as usual. That day he was to drive a goods train from Buxton back to Stockport. This meant taking an engine to Buxton and then having the train made up for the return journey. At the engine shed, Jack and his fireman did all the usual checks and Jack spotted that a steam pipe was leaking so he got a fitter in to fix it. It was a simple job, just tightening a nut. When all was ready off they went.

It was raining when they left the shed but as it grew light the rain cleared and soon they were speeding through the beautiful Derbyshire countryside, which was slowly heaving itself into wakefulness. They were in Buxton by 8 a.m. and the wagons were waiting in the siding. It was a long train – thirty-three wagons loaded with coal, coke, wood pulp, firebricks and pig-iron. At the rear was a guard's van.

The train left Buxton at 11.05 a.m. and was assisted up the incline out of the town by a shunting engine pushing from behind. Even with that help, Jack's engine had to be on full power as well. As they were going up the incline, a wisp of steam came from the pipe which had been repaired earlier. Jack and his fireman bound it round with rags which they kept handy for just such a job. But as they were nearing the top, the pipe burst with a great hiss and the cab was filled with scalding steam. Jack and the fireman were badly burned but tried to turn off the power. However, the steam prevented them from getting anywhere near the controls. The engine, on full power and still being pushed from behind by the shunting engine, approached the top of the hill with no brakes and no way of slowing it! Once it started the descent, it would career on for miles out of control and who knew where it would eventually stop? The outcome was sure to be a disaster whether the train left the rails or crashed into another train.

Jack and the fireman were by now clinging to the outside of the engine – it was the only place away from the steam. Jack ordered his mate to jump. The guard, back in his van, realised something was wrong when the engine breasted the rise and started the descent without slowing, but there was nothing he could do. He was a helpless passenger on a runaway train.

From Bibbington Top down into Whaley Bridge is seven miles and downhill all the way! The engine was on full power, going faster all the time with no way of slowing it. Jack was clinging to the outside of cab. They entered a tunnel and Jack had to grasp close onto the engine to prevent himself from hitting the walls. Then out. They flew through Dove Holes with Jack waving and yelling to attract the attention of the signal box. He hoped they could phone ahead to raise the alarm but the engine was going so fast that he had no idea whether he had been seen or not.

Ahead was the station at Chapel-en-le-Frith. Waiting in the station was a passenger train full of school children and another slow-moving freight train from Rowsley. Jack's train entered the station at 55mph, smashed into the rear of the freight train and then on into the passenger train. Luckily, through Jack's bravery, the Dove Holes signalman had been alerted to the fact that something was wrong and had been able to warn the station ahead. All the passengers had been evacuated. Jack and the guard of the other freight train were killed, but they were the only casualties.

For his bravery in staying on the runaway train and saving the lives of the children on the passenger train, John Axon was awarded a posthumous George Cross.

FIVE

TALES OF ROGUES AND VAGABONDS

English folklore abounds in tales of rogues and vagabonds (and that probably applies to folklore from most other countries too). The common man usually identifies much more with the outlaw and the underdog than with the forces of authority and kings and queens. That is one of the reasons for the popularity of Robin Hood, who might also have been included in this section. However, Robin's fame is so great that I have put him in the heroes section. Most of the outlaws here are anonymous – the little man getting what he thinks are his dues. It overlaps into the simple trickster, and eventually brings us full circle and back round to sheep and 'The Derby Ram'!

THE BUTCHER GETS A TOASTING

In past centuries, writers used to compile lists entitled 'the Wonders of the Peak', which included natural and man-made wonders which they thought visitors to the area should see. These lists varied between three and seven 'wonders' – 'two fonts, two caves, one palace, mount and pit', as one compiler put it. The individual items varied from writer to writer, but always included several from the following: Eldon Hole, Peak Cavern (the Devil's Arse) Pool's Cavern at Buxton, Peverel Castle at Castleton, Mam Tor, the Ebbing and Flowing Well at Tideswell, and Chatsworth House.

Almost all of the lists included Chatsworth, but I much prefer nearby Haddon Hall. It's smaller and more homely. I can imagine myself living at Haddon but not in the pomp of Chatsworth – unless it was as a servant.

We've already had a story about the gentry at Haddon Hall, so here is a very realistic story about life below stairs, although I doubt whether it is really true. It seems to be based on an old song called 'Butter and Cheese and All':

I hadn't been long there sitting, sitting at my ease
When the fire began to melt my butter, likewise to toast
    my cheese,
And every drop that fell in the fire it caused the fire to flare,
And the old man looked up the chimney and he swore
    that Satan was there.

Strange things were happening at Haddon Hall, the Derbyshire home of the Manners family – food was disappear-

ing! Every few weeks, the staff would discover that there
was less butter and cheese than there should be. At first
this was a mystery, but they gradually realised that the loss-
es coincided with visits from a local butcher. This butcher
was called John Taylor. He was a huge man of about eighteen stone and he supplied the house with what was called
'small meat'; that is, the cheap cuts of meat used to feed
the staff rather than the gentry. The butler, on becoming
aware of this suspicion, decided that he would keep a close
eye on Mr Taylor next time he made a delivery.

It was coming up to Christmas time and Haddon was
very busy when John Taylor next arrived. He unloaded his
meat into the kitchen and then the cook showed him into
the adjoining hall. 'Her Ladyship has asked me to wish
you the compliments of the season and to ask you to drink
her health', she said. 'So sit yourself down there by the fire
and I'll bring you a flagon of ale.'

The butcher sat himself down and looked round the
room. At the other side was a table covered with a white
cloth. He crept over and peeked underneath. The table was
laden with parcels of butter and a selection of different
cheeses and other goodies waiting for Her Ladyship's in-
spection before it was put away for Christmas. John Taylor
filled every one of his pockets with packets of butter and
wedges of the various cheeses and then returned to his seat
by the fire, just as the cook brought in his flagon of ale.

The butler had been warned as soon as the butcher arrived and he had been watching all this through a crack
in the door. Now he bounced into the room and patted
Taylor on the back. 'Drink up,' he said, 'and I'll bring you

another glass of ale. It's cold out there today. Come, move your chair up close and I'll throw another log on the fire.'

The butcher could not refuse without arousing suspicion, so he sat by the roaring fire whilst the butter and cheese in his pockets began to melt and run down into his boot.

'My, you're sweating now', said the butler. 'Let me move the chair round so that you can warm your other side!' So the other side of John Taylor was toasted and his other boot was filled with melted butter and bubbling cheese.

When the butler did eventually let him leave, he left very quickly indeed and never stole from Haddon Hall again.

THE DRUNKEN BUTCHER OF TIDESWELL

Tideswell, near Buxton, is famous for its grand church which people call 'the Cathedral of the Peak'. This church was built with the money earned off the backs of sheep, which were an important part of the Derbyshire economy.

Next door to this church lived a butcher. He was a very successful man and made a good living by butchering sheep and cows for the country folk all around. When things were going well there was no one in the neighbourhood he would have changed places with, not those who owned the profitable lead mines, not those with flocks of sheep on the moors, not even the baron in his hall.

This butcher was a very tall, thin man despite his trade and his good living, and that was more surprising because he loved a drink. Every evening he would fill himself with nut brown ale or good red wine – or both! Then, when he went to bed he would snore and grunt contentedly for a good ten hours, if he was allowed to.

There was only one thing that worried this butcher and that was the supernatural – the spirits which danced around in the moonlit hours and the grisly ghosts which he believed cavorted in the neighbouring churchyard once night fell. In the daylight he paid no heed to the dismal tombs and the overgrown graves, but he would not be caught out of his house after nightfall.

Now, one summer's day this butcher mounted his good forest pony and set out to visit a friend. It was partly a business visit and partly social. The friend was Simon the Tanner, who lived in Whaley Bridge, and the butcher had a good cow hide which he knew Simon would be pleased to buy. He was feeling as jaunty as his pony as they trotted over Tideswell Moor, through Sparrow Pit and Paislow Moss, then past Sandy Way Head until he slowed to carefully descend the hill into Chapel-en-le-Frith. When he came into that town he made his way to the Rose of Lancaster to quench the thirst his ride had given him. Outside the inn he found three of his regular drinking companions: the smith, the parson and the pardoner. They hailed him and asked where he was going. 'To Whaley Bridge', he said 'to sell this fine cow hide to Simon the Tanner.'

'Well, you won't go another foot before you've dismounted and taken a sup with me and I've taken a sup with you and then we've both taken a sup with these, our two good companions' said the smith.

'No, I dare not linger,' said the butcher, 'for I swore to my wife that I would not be late home.'

'You should only swear to God, not your wife, so worry not', said the parson.

'But I was drunk last night and if I stay here with you I'll be drunk again tonight.'

'Fear not', said the pardoner. 'Why do you confess that to me? You can get drunk every night and you'll be forgiven as far as I'm concerned!'

So the butcher got down from his horse and they went into the inn and the jolly company drank and drank until the sun started to go down and the stars blinked into the sky. It was now obvious that the butcher was not going to go on to Whaley Bridge and Simon the Tanner would not get the good cow hide that day! As the evening went on the company grew merrier and noisier until eventually they all staggered to their feet, joined hands and danced round singing:

> We've all been drunk on yesternight
> And drunk the night before;
> And so we're drunk again tonight
> If we never get drunk no more…

Then they fell into the street and his friends hoisted the butcher, with great difficulty, onto his horse, slapped its rear and off he galloped into the night. He found it very difficult to stay in the saddle as the horse rushed along. He couldn't see where he was going because all was misty and dancing in front of his eyes. Trees flew by and he was never sure if it was one tree or two, or quite where it was. He'd set the horse towards a gate and then find the gate had moved but, luckily, the horse always found the way through. The very forests seemed to repeat the song from the inn:

> We've all been drunk on yesternight
> And drunk the night before;
> And so we're drunk again tonight
> If we never get drunk no more…

The butcher rode back over Paislow Moss and when he reached Chamber Knowle he was nearly scared out of his skin by the screeching of an owl. He rode by the Forest Wall, scattering the deer browsing on the undergrowth and up the Slack onto Tideswell Moor, where the horse took the bit in its mouth and galloped free and unhindered.

Then the moon came out from behind a cloud and bathed the entire moor with light and the butcher nearly died of fright for there, galloping alongside him, was a phantom horseman – one of those spirits he had always feared. The butcher shrieked in fear and dug his spurs into his horse's flanks. He rode as he had never ridden before. Fear made him as sober as a judge. But however fast the butcher rode, the evil spectre kept pace with him; occasionally a few feet behind, occasionally a few in front, but always matching him pace for pace until, at last, they raced into Tideswell town, past the shadow of the church and skidded to a halt in a cloud of dust at the butcher's door.

'What ails thee, you drunken butcher?' shouted his wife from the bedroom window.

'What ails thee, you drunken butcher?' yelled half the town who had been woken by his headlong flight.

'A ghost! A ghost!' yelled the butcher. 'It raced me over the moor and only disappeared when I reached the shadow of the churchyard wall.'

'A ghost! A ghost!' mimicked his neighbours.

'A ghost! A ghost! You drunken fool!' laughed his wife. 'It was no ghost, it was your own shadow in the moonlight!'

The butcher, feeling rather foolish and very hung-over now the ride and the fright had shaken all the drunkenness out of him, put the horse in the stable and shamefacedly went into the kitchen to meet his wife, who greeted him by pouring a pan of cold water over his head. She gave him a good telling off and made him promise that he would not get drunk with his mates again – a promise he endeavoured to keep, but not wholly successfully.

The story of his ride went round the neighbourhood and it took the butcher many years to live down the night he tried to escape from his own shadow! In fact, he never quite managed to shake the story off and I've made sure he still can't by telling it to you now!

THE BAKEWELL ELEPHANT

This is not a folk tale – yet! It is a true story and a news item, but the events are so bizarre I think it should be better known and become a folk tale – that's why it's included here.

In May 1905 the circus and menagerie belonging to 'Lord' John Sanger & Sons arrived in Bakewell and set itself up on the field by the river, which is now the Showground. (The publicity material made it clear that the circus was not to be confused with that of 'Lord' *George* Sanger, who was both his brother and his rival.) The arrival of the circus was an annual event which the people of Bakewell looked forward to. It arrived with all the pomp and fanfare that was expected, including a procession through the town. Before the show started, everyone looked around the menagerie at all kinds of exotic wild beasts – lions, leopards, camels, bears, wolves and 'horse faced antelopes'. (George's circus even boasted a quagga – a now-extinct animal, halfway between a horse and a zebra.)

The show included all the classic circus acts: clowns, of course; lion tamers and bareback riders; performing dogs and knife throwers; jugglers and fire eaters; acrobats walked the tight rope and trapeze artists flew; but the highlight was the elephants. The elephant herd numbered half a dozen and the leader was a huge male called Old Paul. (Or sometimes, for some reason, Philis!) Old Paul was 9½ft tall and weighed about 4 tons. He had a reputation for being 'difficult' and had previously killed a keeper by kneeling on him, and had injured several more. He was not an animal to mess with.

At the end of the circus show, the practice was for the elephants to return to the ring, where they would be led round to accept gifts from the crowd. They'd reach out with their trunks and gently take sweets, apples and lumps of bread. Everyone loved this. On the night in question, all went well until a child in the audience gave Old Paul a toffee from his pocket; and stuck in this toffee there just happened to be a needle. The boy claimed it was an innocent mistake. He didn't know there was a needle in his pocket and it just happened to get stuck to the toffee… He hadn't meant to do anything bad... He was a good boy…

The boy might have got away with the spiteful trick if it hadn't been Old Paul he gave the sweet to. The needle stuck in the delicate flesh of Old Paul's trunk and the pain caused him to lash out. His trunk caught the keeper, Frank Bailey, across the back, knocking him to the ground, and then Old Paul tried to kneel on him. Luckily for Frank, another elephant pushed Old Paul away and saved his life. Old Paul was led outside.

Up to that point the audience had assumed all this was part of the act and applauded wildly. They changed their minds, though, when the side of the big top was ripped apart and a frenzied elephant came rampaging into the tent, took hold of the main pole in its trunk and started to shake it. They panicked and ran for their lives, and who can blame them? Old Paul was also frightened by the noise and panic and he ran off to Haddon Hill.

What do you do when there is a mad, killer elephant loose in the Derbyshire countryside? You send for the Derbyshire Yeomanry. A firing party arrived and dispatched Old Paul. At the moment Old Paul died, all the other elephants trumpeted so loudly that a boy who was sitting on a nearby fence fell off into the ditch and was injured. And the boy's name? George *Olivant*!

There were no more mishaps and at the end of the week the circus moved on to Buxton, leaving the people of Bakewell with a big health and safety problem – the rotting carcass of a dead elephant. It was decided to take

it away to the town tip at Greenhills (now the Deepdale Business Park) where it could be buried. A crane and horses were sent for. When the crane took the weight and lifted the body, Old Paul trumpeted and, once again, the crowd fled for their lives! But it was only the gasses of putrefaction being released from the body. He was dead.

A few weeks after the burial, trophy hunters dug up the body and cut off souvenirs. If you look in the Old House Museum in Bakewell, you can see one of Old Paul's teeth and one of his feet, which has been made into an umbrella stand. At least four local families claim to have another foot!

> Now the elephant's days are o'er
> He will walk the streets no more.
> He bid farewell to all the show
> On Saturday last they laid him low.

Contemporary verse

THE MAN WHO STOLE THE PARSON'S SHEEP

Long ago, in a little village up in the remotest part of the Peak District, lived a poor man with a large family. He scraped a living doing odd jobs all through the year and they just about got by. But every year, at Christmas time, he made sure his family had a really good feast, for he stole a sheep. Everyone knew this happened, but they could never prove it because the evidence had always disappeared – been eaten – before they could find it. One year the sheep he stole happened to belong to the parson.

One morning soon afterwards this parson happened to be walking down a track near the village when he heard singing. He looked over the dry stone wall and there, playing in the dirt behind the wall, was one of the children from this family – a young lad of eight or nine years old.

The parson listened quietly for a few minutes and what the boy was singing was this:

> My father's stolen the parson's sheep
> So a right good Christmas we shall keep.
> We shall have both pudding and meat
> And he can't do nothing about it.

'I say, lad,' said the parson, 'you've got a lovely voice. You shouldn't keep it a secret, you should let everyone hear. I'll tell you what. Come along to church on Sunday and sing to all the congregation. Then they'll know how well you can sing.'

'Oh, I couldn't do that,' replied the boy, 'I don't know any songs.'

'Well, that little song you were singing then, that will do fine', said the parson.

'No,' said the boy, 'I can't come to church looking like this. My clothes are all ragged and I haven't got any boots to wear.'

'Don't worry about that,' said the parson, 'you just come along. I'll sort you out some clothes and some new boots.'

And that's what happened. The boy arrived at the church early on the next Sunday morning and, before the service,

the parson took him into the vestry and rigged him out in some second-hand clothes and boots. Then at the end of the service, before the congregation left, the parson went up into the pulpit and said, 'Brethren, brethren, before you leave there is something I'd like you to hear. Living in this village is a boy who has a beautiful voice and today he is going to sing for you.'

He beckoned to the boy, who rose from his seat at the back of the church and walked down the aisle. When he reached the front he turned and faced the congregation – everyone from the village all assembled together. He looked up at the parson and smiled an angelic smile. And then he began to sing:

> When I was in the field one day
> I saw the parson kiss a maid,
> He gave me a shilling not to tell
> And these new clothes do suit me well.

THE DEVIL IN THE CHURCH PORCH

Derbyshire was famous for its sheep. Much of it is hill country and sheep were often the only thing a farmer could raise in the higher, most windswept, parts. So, if the farmers raised sheep, the thieves stole sheep!

One evening a man from Calver and his son set out to steal a sheep. He wasn't stupid and he knew that it was best not to commit a crime on his own doorstep, so they went across the fields and followed the river until they came to Baslow.

That was far enough from home, they thought. As they approached Baslow, he warned his son to go quietly because they did not want to attract attention. He didn't want to cross Baslow Bridge because there was a toll gate there and the gate keeper would see them and might be able to recognise them later, so he decided not to raid the pastures across the river but to look this side.

They crept through the village until they came to the church, and the man told his son to wait in the church porch, where no one would see him while he went and looked around for a sheep he could take. The man would then snaffle it and bring it back to the church. His son could then help him by taking turns to carry it back to Calver.

So the son sat himself down in the church porch. It was a long wait and he had no way of passing the time. He couldn't risk a light or someone may have come to investigate and ask what he was doing there. The two thieves had brought with them a bag of hazelnuts to eat on their long walk and the father had left these with the boy so he started to eat them, cracking them with his teeth and throwing down the shells.

In those days, the curfew bell was still rung in many Derbyshire villages. It was an age-old custom which had originally signalled the time when lights and fires should be extinguished to avoid accidental fires at night, but in recent centuries it had become little more than a habit, although it was sometimes a useful habit as benighted travellers, lost in the darkness, could get their bearings from the sound of the bell.

At the appointed time, the sexton of Baslow made his way towards the church to ring the curfew bell. At that time of night he rarely met anyone and everything was usually silent. But this night, as he entered the church-yard, he heard shufflings and mutterings coming from the church porch. Every few minutes there was a crack-ing sound which he couldn't explain. The sexton, de-spite his job, was a superstitious man who loved horror stories. He liked to swap tales with his cronies about the goings-on of witches – a current favourite was of the scandalous events at nearby Bakewell, which they learned of from penny chap books bought on market day. They all knew about local women dancing naked around stone altars up on the moor in honour of the Evil One himself. (They'd all heard these stories, but none of them could ever identify exactly which local women took part in these activities!) He had always been afraid that one day he might come upon the Devil gather-ing up the souls of the departed from the graves in his churchyard. Now it was all happening here in his own church porch, he thought. That must be the Devil him-self cracking the grave stones. He turned and ran to the vicarage and hammered on the door.

The vicar was getting old and suffered from gout. He didn't appreciate being roused from dozing in front of his fire and definitely didn't want to be dragged out into the cold again. He was beginning to feel relaxed after the evening service and he could feel his bed beckoning. But the sexton was frantic. At first the vicar could not under-stand what he was trying to tell him, and when he did he wasn't sure he wanted to know more – the Devil in my church porch? The best thing to do might be to keep my head down and wait until he goes away, he thought. He tried to make the excuse that his gout was so bad that he couldn't hobble across to the church again that night, but the sexton would hear none of it. 'I'll take you on my back', he said. 'You've only got to show yourself and say a blessing and the Devil will flee. Then I can go in and ring the bell.'

So the sexton took the vicar on his back and staggered across to the churchyard gate. They paused and listened and after a minute heard a crack. They both shuddered. Then the sexton crept on nearer the porch.

The boy had now finished the last of the nuts and he stood up and brushed the shells onto the floor, went to the porch entrance and looked out to see if there was any sign of his father coming back. In the darkness he saw the silhouette of the sexton with the vicar on his back just entering the gate and thought it was his father with a sheep.

'My, that's a fat one, we'll have him', he whispered, just loud enough for the person he assumed was his father to hear.

The sexton was terrified. He cried out, 'Yes, he's fat alright and you're welcome to him, but you can't have me!' and he dropped the vicar and ran for his life – or should I say his soul! The vicar was equally scared. He picked himself up and, gout or no gout, he picked up his skirts and leapt over the wall and was back behind the locked door of the vicarage before the boy had even realised it wasn't his father with a sheep.

It was a good hour later that the father did return and he had found a good fat sheep. The boy helped him carry it home and they got there without any trouble.

The next morning the vicar and the sexton armed themselves with crosses and holy water and, holding the Bible before them, they gingerly approached the church porch. All they found was a scattering of hazelnut shells on the floor and a few wisps of sheep's wool caught on the lock. Then they realised that it hadn't been the Devil in their porch the night before and they felt rather foolish and ashamed of themselves, so they both kept quiet and never mentioned the events of that night again.

THE SHEEP THIEF

There were two brothers who made their living by stealing sheep. They were both rough, hard-hearted men who cared nothing for anyone except themselves and thought they had a right to take anything they wanted from anyone. They never gave a second thought to the results of their actions. This made them very unpopular in their neighbourhood. At that time, a man could be hanged for stealing a sheep, but before that could happen there had to be evidence and a hearing before a judge and these two brothers were too clever for that. So the local people decided to take things into their own hands.

One night, on their way home from the local pub, a bit the worse for wear and not aware of what was happening around them, these two brothers found themselves ambushed by a gang of men with their collars turned up and their hats pulled well down over their faces. The brothers had sacks pulled over their heads and their hands were tied behind them so they couldn't escape and they were dragged off to an old barn in the middle of nowhere. When the hoods were taken off their heads, they were confronted with a glowing fire and, in the fire, a branding iron.

Both brothers were branded on their foreheads with the letters 'ST', which stood for 'Sheep Thief' and was meant to show that everyone knew they were sheep thieves and they'd never be able to pretend they weren't sheep thieves. From now on they wouldn't be able to get away with a thing.

The brothers took this in very different ways. One brother felt humiliated and stayed indoors, unable to face the world. It preyed on his mind so much that after a short while he took his own life. The other brother brazened it out. He went about his everyday life much as usual and returned the glares of his neighbours. (But he didn't do any sheep thieving!) But after a while, and after the suicide of his brother, even he gave in to the pressure. He decided that he would move away and start again somewhere else where people didn't know him. Don't get the wrong idea, he wasn't turning over a new leaf and he wasn't giving up his evil ways; he was just looking for somewhere where it would be easier to go about his trade without everyone watching him.

If you are going to make a fresh start you may as well move as far away as you can, so he left his native Derbyshire and moved way down south to Essex. The new place he moved to was almost as remote and quiet as the place he left and the locals were not used to newcomers. They could have been suspicious or antagonistic but they were just interested. They wondered who the newcomer was and why he had come there.

Then, although he tried to cover it up with a kerchief, someone noticed the mark on his forehead. Word went round the village: 'He has the letters ST on his forehead'.

Rumours and theories abounded. Everyone had an idea as to what it might mean – but no one guessed at the correct answer. In fact, the explanation that stuck was that he was a saint! The villagers felt honoured and awed to have their own saint living in the village. The brother did not know about this of course, for he kept himself to himself and didn't hear the gossip. The first he knew of it was when a little deputation of villagers brought him a pan of fine stew and formally welcomed him to their community. 'I've landed on my feet here', he thought.

And then they began to ask him to do strange things: Would he touch the eyes of a blind man? Could he please breathe on a sick child? Would he pray for a barren wife? He didn't know what was going on, but discovered that if he did as he was asked he was rewarded with favours and life was good.

As the years passed he gradually dropped his criminal ways – he had no need of them – and he became an honoured and valued member of his community. And although he never quite became a saint, he was definitely not the blackguard he had been in his young days. When he died, everyone came to his funeral and he was mourned and missed by young and old alike.

And so the moral of the story is: if you treat someone like a thief they will behave like a thief, but if you treat them like a saint, you never know, they just might start to behave like a saint.

And that seems a perfect note on which to finish. That isn't actually an old Derbyshire story. I heard it told by that well known Lake District-based storyteller Taffy Thomas. Taffy was told it by a girl of junior school age. Where she got it from, neither of us know, but I suspect it may have been a story told in a school assembly.

But, whatever its starting point, now it fulfils all the criteria to be considered a true Derbyshire folk tale. The originator has been forgotten. It has been orally transmitted through several tellers and, in the process, has changed and adapted to suit its environment. It fits seamlessly into the existing canon of work and is timeless. And it also has a worthwhile moral!

Bibliography

Llewellyn Jewitt, *The Ballads and Songs of Derbyshire* (Bemrose & Sons, Derby, 1867)

Sidney Oldall Addy, *Household Tales & Traditional Remains, Collected in the Counties of York, Lincoln, Derby & Nottingham* (David Nutt, The Strand, London, and Pawson & Brailsford, Sheffield, 1895)

Thomas Middleton, *Legends of Longdendale, Being a Series of Tales Founded Upon the Folk-Lore of Longdendale Valley and its Neighbours* (First published 1906, reprinted by Longdendale Amenity Society, 1970)

The above are the three main sources for these tales. Most subsequent tellings and collections draw upon them. The Addy seems impossible to get hold of, although various reference libraries hold copies. I was able to buy an old copy of Jewitt quite easily on the internet. The Thomas Middleton is available as an 'on demand' reprint from various internet sites. (This is not, of course, Thomas Middleton the playwright and contemporary of Shakespeare, although 99 per cent of internet book sites assume it is. He would have been very long lived!)

OTHER COLLECTIONS:

Katherine M. Briggs, *Dictionary of British Folk Tales* (Routledge & Kegan Paul Ltd, 1970)

Trevor Brighton, The Discovery of the Peak District (Phillimore, 2004)

R.M. Litchfield, *Strange Tales of the Peak* (Hall & Sons, Derby, Derbyshire Heritage Series, 1992)

Elizabeth Eisenberg, *The Derbyshire Year* (Hall & Sons, Derby, 1989)

Richard Freeman, *Explore Dragons* (Heart of Albion Press, 2006)

Eric Swift, *Folk Tales of the East Midlands* (Thomas Nelson & Sons Ltd, 1954)

Jennifer Westwood & Jacqueline Simpson, *The Lore of the Land* (Penguin, 2005)

RECORDINGS (CDS):

Pete Castle, *Poor Old Horse* (MATS026 2008, includes 'Like Meat Loves Salt')

Pete Castle, *The Jenny & the Frame & the Mule* (MATS023 2000, includes 'Crooker' and 'Spinners & Weavers')

Various Artists, *The Derby Ram* (MATS008 2001, includes two versions of 'The Derby Ram' and a telling by Roy Harris of a different version of 'Hannah Baddeley')

The above recordings are all available on www.petecastle.co.uk